WILDFLOWERS
IN COLOR

Solidago spp.

WILDFLOWERS IN COLOR

ARTHUR STUPKA

WITH THE ASSISTANCE OF

Donald H. Robinson

HarperPerennial

A Division of HarperCollins*Publishers*

Botanical information and photographs were provided by the following organizations:

SHENANDOAH NATURAL HISTORY ASSOCIATION
Eastern National Park and Monument Association
Great Smoky Mountains Natural History Association

FIRST HARPERPERENNIAL EDITION published 1994.

ISBN 0-06-273302-8

94 95 96 97 98 KP 10 9 8 7 6 5 4 3 2 1

CONTENTS

INTRODUCTION

This book embraces the area commonly known as the Southern
Appalachian Mountains. Called by botanists the vegetation cradle of
eastern North America, this region displays in profusion wildflowers
common in much of the eastern United States. Shenandoah National
Park, Blue Ridge Parkway, and the Great Smoky Mountains National
Park are prime undisturbed areas in which to see the diverse native
flora east of the Rocky Mountains. This mountainous region is favored
by a temperate climate. The four seasons that prevail over much of
the eastern United States are well defined with a lengthening of winter
as one ascends the higher peaks. There, at altitudes from about 3,500
to 6,000 feet and above, the colder temperatures and shortened growing season make for climatic conditions approximating those of northern New England and Canada, and this is reflected by the coniferous
forests of spruce and fir. This boreal element, so picturesque to the
layman and so intriguing to the botanist, is a holdover from Pleistocene
times.

It was during the Ice Age that this highland region served as a
haven for the plants and animals that retreated before the great con-
tinental glaciers. As the ice-fettered land again became free some living
things migrated northward while others were left stranded on the higher
mountains where they gradually inched their way upward as the warm-
ing cycle continued. This trend has continued down to our time so
that now only slender interrupted segments of what was once an

vii

unbroken boreal forest remain. In the Shenandoah National Park, where the highest elevation is 4,049 feet (Hawksbill Mountain), there is only a very small remnant of these Canadian Zone flora and fauna; more extensive areas survive along the Blue Ridge Parkway and in the Great Smokies where, although farther to the south, the mountains rise to appreciably higher altitudes.

On the summit of Mt. Mitchell, 6,684 feet above sea level, the Appalachian Mountains reach their highest elevation; this is not far from the Blue Ridge Parkway and approximately twenty airline miles east of Asheville, North Carolina. Clingmans Dome in Great Smoky Mountains National Park, 6,643 feet, is second highest. The southernmost extension of this Canadian life zone in the eastern United States is on the slopes of Clingmans Dome and on Tanasee Bald along the Blue Ridge Parkway. The outliers of the boreal coniferous forest there compare to the evergreen spruce-fir forests that sweep across Canada from the Pacific to the Atlantic coasts. Not only is the red spruce of the high Southern Appalachians identical with that of the far north, but other trees such as yellow birch, mountain ash, mountain maple, and pin cherry are the same, and many shrubs, herbs, and nonflowering plants are identical. With some modifications, therefore, one finds islands of Canadian flora stranded along the higher reaches of these eastern mountains.

In addition to the readily identified habitat called the Canadian Zone, two other life zones can be recognized here: the Transition (also referred to as the Alleghenian) and the Upper Austral (or Upper Carolinian). In a general way the Canadian Zone is that part of the mountains above 4,000 feet; the Transition ranges from 2,500 to 4,000 feet; and the Upper Austral is that part below 2,500 feet. The terms "higher," "middle," and "lower," frequently used in the present account, correspond to these zones. So much overlapping takes place, however, that these zones are often difficult to recognize, especially by persons not well acquainted with these mountains. On the lower slopes the vegetation is akin to the flora of the Piedmont, there being little or no Coastal Plain entities involved.

While natural forces spread over a long period of time have wrought changes in the vegetation of these mountains, recent and rapid changes have taken place as a result of mankind's activities. Logging operations, the clearing of land for homesteading and farming, fires (both natural and man-caused), and grazing were factors in the years prior to the protection that came as a result of national park and parkway designations. Introduction of exotic species of plants was a factor on farms and in gardens. The passing of the American chestnut, one of the most important and most abundant trees in the southern highlands, is a major forest tragedy that is now in its final stages.

Of the three areas with which this account is primarily concerned it is logical that the one with the richest flora is at the southern limits of this long range of mountains. Whereas some nine-hundred kinds of flowering plants are listed for Shenandoah National Park, the number in the Great Smokies is greater by at least 50 per cent. Within this sanctuary of eight-hundred square miles the plants are not only of unusual variety but many are of exceptional size, with a number of shrubs growing to tree proportions and approximately twenty kinds of trees reaching record size. This is the luxuriant region that has attracted foreign plant collectors for two centuries.

The wealth of the flora in these ancient mountains may be attributed in part to its geographical location; here it underwent neither the long submergence by ancient seas nor scouring by Pleistocene ice sheets. Precipitation, which totals 52 inches per year at Big Meadows in Shenandoah National Park, rises to approximately 70 inches at a comparable elevation (3,510 feet) in the Great Smokies; on Clingmans Dome (6,643 feet) this increases to 85 inches. The long growing season at the foot of the mountains decreases in proportion to an increase in altitude until at 5,000 feet or higher the winter season spans about one-half of the year. Hundreds of miles of fast clear streams drain the forested mountain slopes. Although these are the highest ranges in our eastern states they are not high enough for timberline conditions to prevail at this latitude, and therefore a forest-cover clothes the entire region. These are some of the factors contributing to the richness of the Southern Appalachian flora.

All the major categories of flowering plants — trees, shrubs, vines and herbs — are represented by species described in this book. The ratio of the number of kinds of wildflowers in this volume to the number growing in an area such as Great Smoky Mountains National Park may be in the vicinity of 1:5 because of the exclusion of all the grasses, all but one of the sedges, and many of the smaller and more

inconspicuous plants. Then too certain large genera such as blackberries *(Rubus),* violets *(Viola),* goldenrods *(Solidago),* and asters
(Aster) are represented by one or only a few species whereas a dozen
or more of each may occur in the areas. In a few of the taxonomically
"difficult" genera such as hawthorns *(Crataegus)* and blueberries *(Vaccinium)* the comments relate to the group as a whole. Approximately
80 per cent of the plants treated here are to be found in all three areas;
the initials under the plant descriptions are for these three park areas:
Shenandoah (SH), Blue Ridge (BR), and Great Smoky (GS). Figures
are given to show the ratio of the plant to the photograph; for example,
2× means that the plant is twice the size shown.

Ordinarily the farther south one goes, the earlier he may expect
to meet the harbingers of spring. Therefore the vanguard of spring
wildflowers comes to the lower altitudes of the Great Smoky Mountains, and unless the winter season had been exceptionally long and
severe, the month is March. At first the progression of flowering is
slow, but in April the springtime gains such momentum that by the
last week of that month one might list fully two-hundred species of
wildflowers in full bloom. That is the number ordinarily recorded during the annual three-day Spring Wildflower Pilgrimage held in Gat-
linburg, Tennessee, on the last weekend in April.* This popular foray
represents an excellent method for becoming acquainted with wildflowers *in place.*

May and June are also highly recommended as times for visiting
Shenandoah and Great Smoky Mountains National Parks as well as
the Blue Ridge Parkway. It is then that azaleas, mountain laurel, and
rhododendrons are in flower. By July there are few plants with conspicuous flowers at the lower altitudes, but that is a very good time
to visit the cool higher elevations where a fine variety of showy species
come into their prime. By October, of course, although the floral
spectacle is almost over with a few late asters and goldenrods remaining
as though to defy the early frosts, the pageantry of coloring leaves
works its magic throughout the low and middle altitudes. During
most years this spectacle is at or near its peak from October 10 to 20
in Shenandoah National Park and along the parkway, and October
20 to 30 in the Great Smokies.

*Pertinent information is available from the Chamber of Commerce, Gatlin-
burg, Tennessee.

Shenandoah and Great Smoky Mountains National Parks and the Blue Ridge Parkway are sanctuaries administered by the National Park Service. Within these areas all animals, except fishes, are given year-around protection, and no disturbance of the plant life is permitted. As one oldtime ranger phrased this park conservation principle, "Take nothing but pictures, and leave nothing but your footsteps."

ACKNOWLEDGMENTS

As originally written, this book is intended to cover the three inter-connecting National Park Service areas in the Southern Appalachians — Shenandoah National Park, Blue Ridge Parkway, and Great Smoky Mountains National Park. Because of diverse latitudinal and altitudinal factors in this "vegetation cradle," the book's usable range is large, extending north to New England and west to the Mississippi River. The Southern Appalachians is a prolific botanical area because it includes the overlapping zone between many northern and southern species of plants, growing side by side or separated by a few hundred feet of elevation on the steep mountain slopes.

Preparation of this book involved some very complicated coordination among the three parks in obtaining basic information, collecting illustrative material, and arranging for its publication. The interpretive staff of the three areas, namely, Chief Naturalists Ray Schaffner, Donald Robinson, and Ross Bender, planned and set up the publication, with Mr. Robinson acting as coordinator between the areas and the publisher. Regional Naturalist Paul E. Schulz and Publications Officer Roger Rogers, of the National Park Service's Southeast Regional Office, were responsible for working out the initial publication arrangements.

Writer Arthur Stupka, one of the foremost authorities on the botany of the Great Smoky Mountains and adjacent ranges, was formerly Chief Naturalist of Great Smoky Mountains National Park, and has now retired to work on his natural history notes collected over many years, and to write additional publications on the flora and fauna of these southern mountains.

Full credit for the illustrations used here is included at the end of this section, but particular credit should be given to the following, without whose photographic ability and wholehearted cooperation the excellent illustrations included here would not have been possible: Assistant Chief Naturalist David C. Ochsner, of the Blue Ridge Parkway, spent most of his spare time for two consecutive summers searching out and photographing flowers. Mr. Hershal L. Macon, of Knoxville, Tennessee; Mr. William A. Simpson, of East Point, Georgia; and Mr. F. R. Dulany, of Savannah, Georgia, all made their entire collections of wildflower photographs available for use in this book. The collections of all three parks provided most of the remainder, including many under the names credited in the following list.

Many other National Park Service personnel contributed materially to the success of this publication, and to these, whose names are too numerous to include here, we express our appreciation.

Eastern National Park and Monument Association and the Great Smoky Mountains and Shenandoah Natural History Associations furnished the necessary financial backing for the initial publication, including costs of authorship and preparation of materials.

Following is a complete list of photographic contributions, some of which were furnished from the photographer's own files, others coming from the official files of Shenandoah National Park, Blue Ridge Parkway, and Great Smoky Mountains National Park: Leslie Arnberger, William N. Bergen, Donald M. Black, Willard Dilley, F. R. Dulany, Earl W. Estes, Jr., Paul G. Favour, Jr., Henry Heatwole, Craig Heller, W. S. Justice, Henry Lix, Hershal L. Macon, David C. Ochsner, Virginia Phelps, Donald H. Robinson, Ray Schaffner, R. M. Schiele, Jay Shuler, William A. Simpson, University of West Virginia, Ken Thurmond, and Sam P. Weems.

The eighth edition of *Gray's Manual of Botany* (1950) is the authority for the names and arrangement of herbaceous plants and shrubs. *Check List of Native and Naturalized Trees of the United States (Including Alaska)* is the authority for the names of trees.

WILDFLOWERS
IN COLOR

FRASER'S SEDGE   *Cymophyllus fraseri*

Whereas most sedges are small grasslike herbs with inconspicuous flowers, this Southern Appalachian species has numerous straplike leaves and showy flowers. The leaves are thick and glossy and may measure 1–2 in. wide and 2 ft. or more in length. The creamy-white flowers ordinarily appear in April and May. This plant is generally uncommon except in the Great Smoky Mountains where it grows in rich woods and along small watercourses at altitudes of 1,500–4,000 ft.

BR,GS   3×   Sedge family

JACK-IN-THE-PULPIT   *Arisaema triphyllum*

Because of its predominantly green color this plant is often overlooked in the rich woods where it normally grows. It is a common herb at low and middle altitudes where it flowers from April to June. The tube of the spathe, often colored or veined with purple, may be 1–3 in. deep. A showy cluster of glossy red fruit replaces the familiar "Jack" by late summer or autumn. Known also as "Indian turnip," the plant's corm or bulblike root has a sharp taste until cooked.

SH,BR,GS   2×   Arum family

1

DAYFLOWER   *Commelina communis*

A native of Asia, this somewhat fleshy herb now grows in most of the eastern states. The deep blue flowers, approximately ½ in. across, are composed of 3 petals, 2 of which are larger than the third. Dayflowers blossom from June until early autumn, often growing along roadsides and in dooryards at lower altitudes. Other members of its family are mostly natives of tropical regions.

SH,BR,GS   1×   Spiderwort family

VIRGINIA SPIDERWORT   *Tradescantia virginiana*

The 3 blue or purplish flower petals of the Virginia spiderwort are the same size, in contrast to the related dayflower *(Commelina communis)* which it somewhat resembles. Spiderwort flowers, 1–2 in. across, are about double the size of dayflower blossoms, with longer, almost grasslike leaves that are channeled along the middle. The latter may be up to 1 ft. long and ½–1 in. wide. It grows along roadsides, in meadows, and in woods at low and middle altitudes where it flowers from May–August. Its genus name honors John Tradescant, gardener to Charles I, King of England.

SH,BR,GS   2×   Spiderwort family

2

TURKEYBEARD
Xerophyllum asphodeloides

The turkeybeard, a rare plant in the Great Smokies, grows at Linville Falls, Craggy Gardens, and Mileposts 349–350 and near 361 on the Blue Ridge Parkway. (It also occurs in scattered locations near the north end of the parkway and in Shenandoah National Park.) It is a tall (2½–5 ft.) perennial herb whose very narrow leaves grow in grasslike clumps. The numerous white scentless flowers, arranged in a 3–6 in. long cluster, 2–3 in. in diameter, expand first at the bottom. It flowers from May into early summer. Indians occasionally used leaves of this plant to weave baskets.

SH,BR   6×   Lily family

BLAZING-STAR   *Chamaelirium luteum*

The numerous small white flowers of blazing-star are arranged in a narrow spikelike cluster 3–9 in. long. Ordinarily the plant grows 1–2 ft. high, but taller ones sometimes occur. It usually flowers from April to July. This herb is fairly common in moderately rich woodlands and in meadows at low to middle altitudes. It is also called "devil's-bit" or "fairy-wand."

SH,BR,GS   3×   Lily family

3

FLY-POISON
Amianthium muscaetoxicum

With its dense terminal cluster of white flowers and the numerous grass-like leaves arising mostly from its base, fly-poison is an attractive plant, somewhat similar to turkeybeard, but with a smaller flower cluster. It grows from 1½–4 ft. tall. The compact flower cylinder, 2–6 in. long, turns yellowish to greenish with age. This herb, fairly common along the Parkway and in Shenandoah, is restricted to the eastern end of the Great Smokies, where it blooms from May to July. Its roots and leaves contain a very toxic alkaloid poisonous to cattle. It is also called "crow-poison."

SH,BR,GS   3×   Lily family

WHITE HELLEBORE *Veratrum viride*

This tall leafy herb produces a loosely branched cluster of flowers that may be 8–20 in. long, but since the blossoms (May–August) are greenish or greenish-yellow they may be overlooked, especially since it usually grows in the shade of high-altitude forests. The strongly veined leaves of this plant may be 5–12 in. long and 3–6 in. wide. "Indian poke" and "itchweed" are other names for it. Its very poisonous roots, when dried and powdered, are used in the manufacture of certain insecticides.

SH,BR,GS   6×   Lily family

4

LARGE FLOWERED BELLWORT
Uvularia grandiflora

Rich woods are the habitat of this large, drooping, single-flowered bellwort. The scentless lemon-yellow blooms, 1–1½ in. long, appear from April to June. The stem, 20–30 in. high, appears to pierce the leaves. A covering of short hairs on the under-surface of the leaves distinguishes large-flowered bellwort from its close relative sessile-leaved bellwort (*U. sessilifolia*). This is a fairly common wildflower at low and middle altitudes.

SH,BR,GS   6×   Lily family

WILD ONION   *Allium cernuum*

Along the Parkway where both this plant and "ramp" or "wild leek" (*A. tricoccum*) grow, wild onion may be distinguished by the presence of leaves at the time of flowering (early summer) and by the nodding, flat-topped flower cluster. The leaves of wild onion are 6–16 in. long and under ¼ in. wide. The flowers—pink, purplish-pink, or white—are borne on stems 8 in. to more than 2 ft. high in July and August. This pungent herb also grows at high altitudes on rocky hillsides.

BR   4×   Lily family

5

RAMP; WILD LEEK *Allium tricoccum*

The leaves of ramp, unlike those of wild onion *(A. cernuum),* are absent in early summer when this odorous plant is in flower. The white flower clusters are held erect on stems 6–15 in. tall. It grows in rich woodlands at elevations up to 5,200 ft. Leaves, 4–12 in. long and 1–2 in. wide, appear early in the spring. It is then that large quantities of these strong-scented herbs are gathered for food by the native people in the vicinity of the Great Smokies, and an annual "Ramp Festival" is held, usually in late April.

BR,GS   1×   Lily family

COMMON ORANGE DAY-LILY   *Hemerocallis fulva*

This tall yellow- or orange-flowered herb, a native of Europe and Asia, is a familiar plant along roadsides, in meadows, and near old homesites and cemeteries. The stems are 2–5 ft. tall and the erect funnel-like flowers (May–August) are 4–5 in. long. The acutely tipped leaves measure 1–2 ft. long and ½–⅔ in. wide. Both the common and scientific names refer to the brief lifespan of the flowers, "beautiful for a day."

SH,BR,GS   1½×   Lily family

Wood lily   *Lilium philadelphicum*

A plant of dry woodlands and clearings, this native lily is rare in these areas. The stem, 1–3 ft. tall, holds 1–5 handsome, erect, reddish-orange flowers. These are 2–4 in. high, spotted purple within. Two to 6 whorls or circles of leaves, 3–8 per whorl, are arranged along the stem. There are more than 2,000 species in the cosmopolitan family to which the wood lily belongs. Included are *Yucca,* the familiar onion *(Allium),* asparagus *(Asparagus),* and tulip *(Tulipa).*

SH,BR,GS   1⅓ ×   Lily family

Turk's-cap lily   *Lilium superbum*

Few families of plants have more attractive flowers than the lilies. This is especially true of the tall turk's-cap which may have 10–40 blossoms on top of a stem 3–8 ft. high. The orange or orange-red flowers have strongly recurved, spotted petals and sepals 2–4 in. long. Unlike day-lily and wood lily, turk's-cap flowers are "nodding" or drooping. The whorled leaves, pointed at both ends, may be 2–6 in. long and ¼–1½ in. wide. This liy is most plentiful at the higher altitudes, where it blossoms in July and August.

SH,BR,GS   4×   Lily family

CAROLINA LILY   *Lilium michauxii*

Although this lily resembles the turk's-cap, it is much shorter (1–3 ft.) and usually grows in drier places. Carolina lily is often 1-flowered or 1–3-flowered in contrast to the many-flowered turk's-cap. The nodding orange-red sepals and petals are often so strongly recurved that the tips overlap each other. The leaves, scattered or in whorls, are 1½–4 in. long. The usual habitats are pine and oak woods at altitudes up to approximately 4,000 ft. It is also known as "Michaux's lily."

SH,BR,GS   4×   Lily family

YELLOW ADDER'S-TONGUE   *Erythronium americanum*

This is a common to abundant wildflower, especially in the high, cool, moist spruce-fir forests. The single, yellow, lilylike flowers are scentless or nearly so. The 6 segments of the flower (3 petals and 3 petal-like sepals, as in most lilies) are often spotted at the base. Leaves are 3–8 in. long and ¾–2 in. wide, smooth, shining, often mottled, and narrowed at the base. At low altitudes the plant blooms in March and April; at high elevations, in May and June.

SH,BR,GS   1½×   Lily family

8

SILKGRASS   *Yucca filamentosa*

Although this plant of many names (Spanish-bayonet, beargrass, Adam's-needle, and curly-hair) is associated with the southwestern United States, up to 6 native species of *Yucca* are listed for the southeastern coastal plain. Silkgrass invades old fields, farmsteads, and dry pinelands in the Southern Appalachian region where its numerous white flowers, borne on tall, woody stems, appear May–July. The long (12–30 in.), narrow, sharp-pointed leaves have twisted, thread-like filaments along their margins, accounting for its specific scientific name *filamentosa*. Shenandoah National Park reports only *smalliana*, a similar-appearing species.

BR,GS   10×   Lily family

BLUEBEAD-LILY   *Clintonia borealis*

At high altitudes in the cool Canadian Zone forests of New England and southward to the Great Smoky Mountains this is a common plant. Its lilylike flowers, ¾–1 in. long, unfurl in May and June. Unlike flowers of the closely related speckled wood-lily *(C. umbellulata)* bluebead-lily flowers are drooping and pale yellow. Also speckled wood-lily bears black berries while bluebead-lily has blue or porcelain-blue berries. The thin leaves of bluebead-lily, usually arranged in 3's, are 5–10 in. long and 1½–3 in. wide.

SH,BR,GS   3×   Lily family

9

SPECKLED WOOD-LILY
Clintonia umbellulata

In May and June speckled wood-lily or "white Clintonia" displays a rounded cluster of erect white flowers that are often dotted with green and purple. Two–4 basal leaves, oblong or oval, are 1½–4 in. wide. In late summer it bears black spherical fruits, about ¼ in. in diameter. This plant grows in woodlands from the low altitudes to approximately 4,000 ft. Its generic scientific name commemorates the eminent DeWitt Clinton (1769–1828). Differences between this and the related bluebead-lily *(C. borealis)* are mentioned under that species.

BR,GS,SH   4×   Lily family

FALSE SPIKENARD   *Smilacina racemosa*

Many small, white blossoms make up the terminal flower cluster of this common woodland species. The flowers (late April–June) are followed by numerous purple speckled reddish berries (July–August). Flower and fruit clusters (1–4 in. long) are on a somewhat zigzag stem (1–3 ft. long), whose alternate leaves, 3–6 in. long, have prominent veins. Ringlike scars of former stems are spaced irregularly along the fleshy rootstock. This perennial is also called "False Solomon's-seal."

SH,BR,GS   3×   Lily family

FALSE OR WILD LILY-OF-THE-VALLEY   *Maianthemum canadense*

This attractive little member of the lily family grows in cool, moist, high-altitude forests. Its stalk of white flowers appears in late May and June. Small clusters of speckled, pale red berries follow in late summer. There may be 1–3 leaves (usually 2) 1–3 in. long, glossy, and somewhat heart shaped. This low creeping perennial grows at altitudes up to 6,000 ft. in the Great Smokies. "Two-leaved Solomon's seal," "elf feather," and "Canada mayflower" are other names for it.

SH,BR,GS   1⅓ ×   Lily family

ROSY TWISTED-STALK   *Streptopus roseus*

This relative of Solomon's-seal is distinguished by leafy zigzag stems. Small rose or purplish flowers appear in May and June usually singly, but occasionally in pairs. Thin, alternately arranged leaves, 2–4 in. long, have a fringe of fine hairs along the margins. In late summer the ripe, round, cherry-red berries, ⅓ in. in diameter, are quite attractive. Rosy twisted-stalk, also called "rose mandarin," grows in cool moist woods at high altitudes.

SH,BR,GS   1⅓ ×   Lily family

11

SOLOMON'S-SEAL   *Polygonatum biflorum*

In rich woods at low and middle altitudes the small nodding flowers of Solomon's-seal appear beneath a slender, gracefully arching stem from April to June. These tubular greenish-yellow blooms, ⅓–½ in. long, usually occur in pairs, often obscured by the oval, pointed leaves. Ranging from 2–4 in. long and ½–2 in. wide, the alternately arranged leaves have prominent veins above and below. The fruit is a dark round berry approximately ¼ in. in diameter. Numerous joints or "knees" along the rootstock are scars resulting from the death of the stalks of previous years.

SH,BR,GS   1×   Lily family

LILY-OF-THE-VALLEY   *Convallaria montana*

This rare wildflower occurs in the Rocky Knob and Sharp Top areas of the parkway, but in the Great Smokies it is very scarce. It closely resembles the related European species. The 2 or 3 strongly veined leaves are 5–12 in. long and 1–2½ in. wide. A 4–9 in. stem bears a one-sided stalk of white flowers, approximately ¼ in. long, in May and June. These nodding blooms, noted for their delightful fragrance, are succeeded by red berries. Another species. *Convallaria majalis,* occurs in Shenandoah. This is a native of Europe that has escaped from old homesites to become "naturalized."

BR,GS   1½ ×   Lily family

12

INDIAN CUCUMBER-ROOT
Medeola virginiana

In moist woods at low and middle altitudes the slender Indian cucumber-root is a common plant over much of the eastern United States. The stem, 1–2½ ft. long, supports two whorls or circles of leaves. The upper whorl has 3–5 leaves, the leaves (4–10) of the lower whorl are somewhat larger. A few (2–9) small, nodding, yellowish-green flowers appear immediately beneath the upper whorl of leaves in May and June. Flowerless plants have but a single terminal whorl of leaves. The round bluish or purplish berries, ¼–½ in. in diameter, ripen in September. The brittle rootstock, 1–3 in. long, tastes like cucumber, hence its common name.

SH,BR,GS   2×   Lily family

ERECT TRILLIUM

Trillium erectum

Three petals + 3 sepals + 3 leaves = *Trillium* (3). Thus the very appropriate scientific name is also the common name of this group of the lily family. The petals of erect trillium may be purplish-red or, in the Great Smokies, mostly white. Pink or greenish-yellow forms occur infrequently. Due to its unpleasant scent, this plant is sometimes known as "stinking Willie." Another of its many names is "wake-robin." It grows in rich woods at practically all altitudes. It flowers from March–June.

SH,BR,GS   1½ ×   Lily family

13

LARGE-FLOWERED TRILLIUM   *Trillium grandiflorum*

One of our most handsome trilliums, it is common and popular over much of its range. The pure white flower turns pink or rose before it fades. It grows in rich woods at altitudes up to 5,000 ft. Large-flowered trillium is 8–18 in. high, and the stem bears a 2–3 in. flower. The fruit, black when ripe, is a spherical berry ¾–1 in. in diameter. Many steep, forested mountainsides are carpeted by the blossoms of thousands of these lovely wildflowers from mid-April into June.

SH,BR,GS   4×   Lily family

PAINTED TRILLIUM   *Trillium undulatum*

Painted trillium is one of the loveliest members of this genus. In May and June the 8–20 in. stem bears a wavy-margined white flower marked with magenta stripes. In August this becomes a very attractive, shining, bright red berry. This plant grows in acid soils at middle and high altitudes in cool moist woods—in some places as high as 6,000 ft.

BR,GS   2×   Lily family

14

COLIC-ROOT *Aletris farinosa*

This rather uncommon plant is similar to some of the ladies'-tresses orchids *(Spiranthes)*. Colic-root has a spikelike cluster of small whitish or cream-colored flowers on a stem 12–40 in. tall. At the base of the stem is a rather dense rosette of narrow, long-pointed leaves 2–6 in. long and ¼–¾ in. wide. These leaves are often a yellowish-green. The species grows in open pinelands and dry sandy woods at the lower altitudes. The granular or mealy appearance of the flowers accounts for its specific name, *farinosa* ("farina" or "starchlike").

BR,GS   3×   Lily family

HAIRY STARGRASS *Hypoxis hirsuta*

The earliest of the bright yellow 6-rayed flowers of hairy stargrass may appear in late April, but this small herb continues to bloom throughout the summer. The stem that supports the rounded cluster of 1–7 flowers is 2–6 in. tall. The few grasslike basal leaves are usually longer than the flowering stem. A common plant of meadows and open woods, it grows in rather dry sandy soils at low and middle altitudes. The Amaryllis family also includes the widely cultivated narcissus of Europe and the spider-lily *(Hymenocallis)* and zephyr-lily *(Zephyranthes)* of the southeastern states.

SH,BR,GS   1×   Amaryllis family

15

NARROW-LEAVED BLUE-EYED GRASS
Sisyrinchium angustifolium

In moist fields and meadows at lower to middle elevations this little iris displays small violet-blue scentless flowers from May–July. The yellow-centered blossoms comprise 3 petals and 3 similar-appearing petal-like sepals, each of which terminates in a sharp abrupt point. It is not a grass, but its winged stems and narrow grasslike leaves 4–20 in. high account for its common name. In the proper habitat it grows very abundantly.

SH,BR,GS   1×   Iris family

CRESTED DWARF IRIS   *Iris cristata*

Along streams and roadsides and on hillsides and bluffs this gregarious little iris is a common plant at the lower altitudes. In April and May it bears blue or purple—rarely pure white (albino)— flowers, quite large for so small a plant. The slender, bright green leaves are 4–9 in. long and average about ½ in. wide. Other species of iris come in many colors—blue, violet, red, yellow, white—thus accounting for the Greek name, iris, meaning "rainbow." Only a few native species grow in the mountains, but close to 100 occur in the low swamplands of the southeastern states.

BR,GS   1⅓ ×   Iris family

16

SMALL YELLOW LADY'S-SLIPPER
Cypripedium calceolus parviflorum

The orchids are a cosmopolitan family of plants comprising several thousand species. They are most plentiful in tropical regions where many of them derive their nourishment chiefly from the air rather than the soil. Some, like coral-root, are largely overlooked because they are so tiny and inconspicuously colored. Small yellow lady's-slipper and a closely related larger-flowered form are among our showiest wild orchids. Ordinarily they grow in rich woodlands at elevations up to about 4,000 ft. They flower from late April into June. They are not common, but may be locally abundant where they do occur.

SH,BR,GS   3×   Orchis family

STEMLESS LADY'S-SLIPPER
Cypripedium acaule

It is the plant, not the flower, of this lovely orchid that is stemless. The blossom stem arises directly from the ground. As orchids go, it is a fairly common wildflower, especially in dry, pine-dominated forests at low and middle altitudes where it begins to bloom in late April. The purplish-pink pouch, or slipper, is veined with crimson. It may reach a length of 2 in., thus making it one of the largest of any of our wild orchid flowers. The 2 basal leaves are 6–8 in. long and 2–3 in. wide.

SH,BR,GS   2×   Orchis family

17

SHOWY ORCHIS   *Orchis spectabilis*

At the southern limits of its range this lovely little orchid begins to flower in late April. Three to 12 flowers bloom on a terminal spike. These, approximately an inch long, are purple above and white below. At the base of the 5-angled stem are 2 thick, glossy, egg-shaped leaves, about half as wide as they are long. This orchid is common in rich woods at low and middle altitudes. Its period of peak blossoming usually marks the time when the great array of spring wildflowers is at its best in the Southern Appalachian Mountains.

SH,BR,GS   1×   Orchis family

YELLOW FRINGED ORCHIS   *Habenaria ciliaris*

This common tall-growing orchid is at its peak bloom in midsummer. A stem 1–2½ ft. tall carries a many-flowered spike of orange (occasionally yellow) blossoms with deeply fringed lips. Along the lower portion of the stem, the lancelike leaves measure 4–8 in. long and ½–1½ in. wide; those higher up are much smaller. This handsome wildflower grows in meadows, open woods, and on fairly dry mountainsides at low and middle altitudes. In some places it is called "orange-plume."

SH,BR,GS   1×   Orchis family

18

LARGE PURPLE FRINGED ORCHIS
Habenaria fimbriata

This tall handsome plant and its close relative, small purple fringed orchis (*H. psycodes*), although regarded as distinct species by many botanists, are very similar. Both have very fragrant lilac-pink or lilac-purple flowers, the lower lip of which is 3-parted and deeply fringed, and both grow in essentially the same habitat (wet meadows and along streams). The large purple fringed appears to be a big counterpart of the smaller orchid in many respects, and they are known to hybridize. Stems of the larger form range from 1–5 ft. high. June–August are the principal flowering months.

SH,BR,GS   3×   Orchis family

SPREADING POGONIA
Cleistes divaricata

In some parts of the coastal plain this orchid is so abundant that large areas turn pale rose when it flowers. But in the Southern Appalachians, this lovely wildflower is rare. Here it usually grows on dry forested slopes from the lowest altitudes up to approximately 4,000 ft., blooming from late May into July. The solitary flowers, 1–1½ in. long, are pale pink. The stem, 1–2 ft. tall, bears a single clasping leaf near its middle.

BR,GS   2½×   Orchis family

19

NODDING LADIES'-TRESSES
Spiranthes cernua

Oakes Ames, one of the greatest authorities on orchids, called ladies'-tresses *(Spiranthes)* "the most perplexing orchid genus in our flora." Not only do the species tend to hybridize readily, but plants growing in the mountains may differ in size and appearance from the same species on the coast. Of the several kinds of these orchids, nodding ladies'-tresses are the latest to flower (August–November) and, usually, the most plentiful. The fragrant flowers, pure white or cream-colored, are arranged or "braided" in 3 or 4 rows. This plant with erect stems 8–18 in. tall, usually grows in colonies on moist grassy banks and meadows and on springy slopes at elevations up to 6,000 ft.

SH,BR,GS   1×   Orchis family

DOWNY RATTLESNAKE-PLANTAIN
Goodyera pubescens

While this orchid somewhat resembles nodding ladies'-tresses *(Spiranthes cernua)*, the handsome basal rosette of evergreen, netted-veined leaves is distinctive. These leaves are 1–2½ in. long and almost an inch wide with an intricate white network against their bluish-green color—a year-around trade-mark of the species. The numerous white flowers, ¼ in. or smaller, are arranged along a stem 6–20 in. tall. It grows in woodlands from the lowest altitudes up to approximately 4,000 ft., flowering during July and August.

SH,BR,GS   4×   Orchis family

20

SPOTTED CORAL-ROOT
Corallorhiza maculata

Brownish or purplish, with no green foliage, and with a stalk of very small flowers, this inconspicuous woodland orchid is often overlooked. The white lip of the flower is spotted with red or purple and the rootstock is branching and coral-like—hence its name. The stem of this orchid may be 8–20 in. tall, but its leaves are merely small scales. This plant often grows in colonies in rather dry woods where it flowers from July into September.

SH,BR   1×   Orchis family

LILY-LEAVED TWAYBLADE   *Liparis lilifolia*

This little orchid grows in rocky woods where its delicate flowers appear from late May to July. The upper limit of its range in the mountains is near 3,000 ft. The pair of basal leaves accounts for the name "twayblade," or "two-blade." These, glossy and light green, clasp the stem with a partial mid-rib. On a stem 4–10 in. tall the mauve or delicate purple flowers are arranged in a loose cluster. For one in search of plant rarities, the discovery of a lily-leaved twayblade is always a thrilling event.

SH,BR,GS   3×   Orchis family

21

PUTTY-ROOT — *Aplectrum hyemale*

From the bulblike roots of this orchid a sticky paste was made with which broken pottery could be mended—hence the name "putty-root." The solitary corrugated basal leaf is one of its most distinctive characteristics. The oval, bluish-green leaf, 4–6 in. long by 1–3 in. wide, remains green throughout the winter and accounts for the species name *hyemale,* meaning "of winter." By May when the plant begins to flower, the leaf disappears. Putty-root inhabits rich rocky woods where, in some areas, it is fairly common.

SH,BR,GS   4×   Orchis family

OILNUT — *Pyrularia pubera*

This as a common shrub in the Southern Appalachian forests, especially where oaks are dominant at elevations up to 4,000 ft. The inconspicuous, small, greenish flowers usually bloom from late April through May. Later in the summer a pear-shaped fruit develops, about the size of a small hickory-nut. The fruit and other parts of the plant contain a poisonous oil and should never be eaten. One botanist claims that the fruit is so oily it would burn like a candle if a wick were drawn through it. "Tallow-nut" and "buffalo-nut" are other names for it. This straggling shrub is said to be parasitic upon roots of rhododendron and possibly other plants.

BR,GS   1×   Sandalwood family

22

CANADA WILD GINGER   *Asarum canadense*

 The pungently aromatic rootstock of this plant gives it its name. It grows abundantly
in rich soils on rocky hillsides at altitudes up to 3,000 ft. The paired kidney-shaped
leaves, 3–6 in. across, are covered by minute hairs. During April or May a solitary low-
growing flower appears, often somewhat concealed by the leaf litter on the forest floor.
It is essentially a cup-shaped calyx of a dull brownish-purple color with three acutely
pointed divisions. This is actually a flower without petals.

SH,BR,GS   ½ ×   Birthwort family

DUTCHMAN'S PIPE   *Aristolochia durior*

 One of the most characteristic plants of the splendid cove-hardwood forests of the
Southern Appalachians is this ropelike woody vine with its big valentine-shaped leaves.
On occasions it climbs fully 100 ft. into the crowns of some of the largest trees. Its
upper altitudinal limit is near 4,800 ft. Flowers appear from late April into June. These
are brownish-purple and strongly curved into the shape of an S, like a Dutchman's-
pipe. Due to its handsome foliage, this vine has been naturalized well outside its native
range.

BR,GS   1×   Birthwort family

POKEWEED   *Phytolacca americana*

A smooth, robust, succulent plant, pokeweed grows over an area extending from Canada to Mexico. It is a large perennial herb 3–10 ft. tall with somewhat flabby leaves and a rather unpleasant odor. Along the edges of cultivated fields, in waste places, on recently cleared land, and elsewhere this common plant may become a troublesome weed. Its large parsnip-like root and glossy black berries are poisonous when eaten by man or farm animals. In early spring the young shoots, *without the roots,* are used to make "poke salad" after being boiled in 2 waters, the first is poured off. Flowers appear from May until frost.

SH, BR, GS   3× Pokeweed family

SPRING-BEAUTY   *Claytonia virginica*

In the higher mountains, it is not unusual for late snowfalls to blanket the forest floor when countless numbers of these little white or pale pink wildflowers are in bloom. Veins of dark pink enhance the beauty of the simple 5-rayed flower. Two leaves rise from a rootlike tuber deep in the ground. They are almost grasslike in the narrow-leafed species *(C. virginica)* and up to an inch wide in the wide-leafed spring beauty *(C. caroliniana).*

SH,BR,GS   1× Purslane family

24

GREAT CHICKWEED

Stellaria pubera

Although the white flowers of this native chickweed are only ⅓–½ in. broad, they are appreciably larger than those of the better-known common chickweed *(S. media)* which is a cosmopolitan weed of European origin. The 5 petals that make up the blossom of great chickweed are so deeply notched that a superficial examination of this flower gives the impression there are 10 instead of 5 petals. The stem may be 4–12 in. tall, and the oblong opposite leaves are ½–2½ in. long. This is a plant of rich woodlands where it often grows in mats from the lowest altitudes to 4,500 ft. Flowers appear in April and May.

SH,BR,GS   1⅓ ×   Pink family

BLADDER-CAMPION   *Silene cucubalus*

The inflated calyx of this European immigrant accounts for its rather distinctive appearance. About ½ in. long, the rounded, conspicuously-veined part of the structure directly beneath the flower appears swollen. The flowers, ½–¾ in. wide, are white (rarely pinkish) and are disposed in loosely branched clusters, their 5 petals so deeply cleft that they look double. Growing mostly along roadsides and in fields and waste places, bladder-campion has a stem 6–20 in. high with variable sized, opposite leaves. It flowers from June to August. This is not a common plant in the Southern Appalachians, but is very conspicuous where it does occur.

SH,BR,GS   1 ×   Pink family

STARRY CAMPION *Silene stellata*

This plant, like its relative bladder-campion *(S. cucubalus)*, has an inflated calyx, but which is not so pronounced. The white flowers, about ¾ in. broad, are scattered in a loosely branched cluster; they have 5 deeply fringed petals. All except the lowest and highest leaves are arranged in whorls of 4 along the stem. These are 2–4 in. long and ½–1 in. wide. The stems are quite rough, and the entire plant is covered with minute hairs. This is a wildflower of woods and shaded banks where it blossoms from June through August.

SH,BR,GS   2×   Pink family

FIRE-PINK

Silene virginica

This attractive star-shaped blossom adds its fiery crimson color to certain dry areas along roadsides from April throughout the spring. Banks, rocky cliffs, and hillsides are its habitat. Beneath the 5-petaled flower is a sticky, elongated calyx, which explains the name "catch-fly" sometimes given this wildflower. The slender, weak stem may be 1–2 ft. tall. In the southern mountains it grows at elevations up to 5,000 ft. where the flowering period may extend well into the summer. The familiar cultivated carnation is a member of the same family.

SH,BR,GS   1×   Pink family

BOUNCING-BET *Saponaria officinalis*

This European immigrant is a plant of roadsides, waste places, railway embankments, and pastures, where it occasionally becomes a persistent weed, spreading by underground rootstocks. In mid-summer, a stout stem, 1–2 ft. tall, bears white or pinkish 5-petaled flowers arranged in dense terminal clusters. The opposite leaves, 2–3 in. long and an inch wide, are strongly ribbed. "Soapwort," one of its many names, comes from the property the roots have of producing a soapy lather with water. This foamy solution was the pioneer's substitute for soap in cleaning silks and woolens.

SH,BR,GS   3×   Pink family

DEPTFORD PINK *Dianthus armeria*

This attractive little plant, a native of the Old World, is generally uncommon in the southern mountains, but fairly plentiful where it does occur. The stiff stem, 8–24 in. tall, bears a terminal cluster of small pink or rose flowers. On close examination the 5-petaled flowers are found to be dotted with white and the petal margins toothed. The leaves are oppositely arranged on the stem, erect, 1–3 in. long, and very narrow. This inconspicuous little pink grows along roadsides and in dry places where it flowers throughout the summer.

SH,BR,GS   ½×   Pink family

27

FRAGRANT WATER-LILY

Nymphaea odorata

This attractive aquatic plant is not commonly seen in the southern mountains where ponds, lakes, and slow-flowing streams are scarce. When not in flower it is easily identified by its large (4–12 in. in diameter), round, floating leaves that are a shining green above and purple below; these rise from a thick horizontal rootstock. The blossoms are usually present from June into September; they are large (3–6 in. across), white or pinkish, and very fragrant, with numerous petals radiating out from a center of yellow stamens. Fragrant water-lilies range from Newfoundland to Florida.

BR   2×   Water-lily family

HISPID BUTTERCUP

Ranunculus hispidus

Buttercups are practically cosmopolitan, ranging from the Arctic regions to the tropics and from near sea level to near summits of our highest mountains. Of approximately 275 species, about a dozen grow in the Southern Appalachian Mountains. The earliest of these to flower, usually in March, is the hispid buttercup, which is small and quite hairy when the 5-petaled yellow blossoms appear. These flowers, ½–1½ in. wide, have petals with smooth edges or only slightly notched at the tip. The 3–5 divided leaves are on a stem that may be 1–2 ft. in length. Occurs upward to 6,000 ft.

SH,BR,GS   1×   Crowfoot family

28

TASSEL-RUE
Trautvetteria caroliniensis

A rather uncommon plant, tassel-rue partly resembles such better-known herbs as baneberry *(Actaea)*, meadow-rue *(Thalictrum)*, and bugbane *(Cimicifuga)*—all in the same family. In fact, tassel-rue is also known as "false bugbane," and at one time was classified as *Cimicifuga*. The small (¼-½ in. wide) white flowers lack true petals but have 3–5 petal-like sepals, borne on stems 2–3 ft. tall. The lobed leaves are 6–8 in. wide and 4–5 in. long; the 5–11 palm-shaped lobes are pointed and sharply toothed. Tassel-rue grows in the woods at altitudes up to 6,000 ft. It flowers from June to August.

SH,BR,GS   2×   Crowfoot family

TALL MEADOW-RUE
Thalictrum polygamum

This is a fairly common plant of the lower altitudes where it may reach heights of 3–10 ft. in wet meadows. While petals are lacking in the flower, the stamens are so numerous and arrayed in such attractive tassels that the large, loosely branched greenish-white clusters of flowers are quite showy. Summer is the flowering season. The oval-shaped leaves, light green above and pale beneath, have 3 blunt lobes. This is the tallest-growing of the several species of meadow-rues that are found in the Southern Appalachian region. It is also called "muskrat weed," "musquash-weed," and "musket-weed."

SH,BR,GS   4×   Crowfoot family

29

RUE-ANEMONE   *Anemonella thalictroides*

The resemblance of the compound basal leaves of this common little wildflower to those of meadow-rue account for both its common and scientific names (rue and *thalictroides*). These broadly oval or round leaves usually have 3 lobes at the end. Rue-anemone displays its clusters of white (rarely pink) flowers in rich woods in April and May. Like wood anemone *(Anemone quinquefolia)*, with which it has been confused, rue-anemone has no true petals, but the sepals are petal-like. This delicate, slender-stemmed plant grows at low and middle altitudes.

SH,BR,GS   1½ ×   Crowfoot family

ROUND-LOBED LIVERLEAF   *Hepatica americana*

Both the round-lobed *(Hepatica americana)* and the sharp-lobed liverleafs *(H. acutiloba)* occur in the southern mountains where they range at altitudes up to about 3,500 ft. in rich woods. While the lobes of the leaves are rounded in the former species they are pointed in the latter—otherwise these plants are quite similar. Intermediate forms have been reported. The petal-like sepals may be white, blue, pink, or lavender; ordinarily they appear in March and April. The rather thick 3-lobed leaves persist through the winter and new leaves make their appearance after the flowering season.

SH,BR,GS   1 ×   Crowfoot family

WOOD ANEMONE
Anemone quinquefolia

According to an ancient elegy, anemones sprang up where the tear drops shed by Venus, for the death of the fair Adonis, struck the earth. It is not too surprising to come upon such a fanciful tale for such a delicate plant. The slender stem of the wood anemone or "windflower," as it is often called, bears a solitary blossom of 4–9 oval-shaped, white, petal-like sepals, often with a pink or purple cast beneath. The species name, *quinquefolia*, refers to the 5-parted (quinque-) basal leaves (folia). It is a spring wildflower whose habitat is the low- and middle-altitude woodlands.

SH,BR,GS 1⅓ × Crowfoot family

VIRGIN'S-BOWER   *Clematis virginiana*

Not all 3-leaved vines should be avoided like poison ivy, and the harmless virgin's-bower is a good example. In August, its flowering peak, masses of creamy-white blossoms make this a most handsome native plant. Some flowers appear in July and into September. This is mostly a vine of lowland areas (to 2,500 ft.) where it climbs over shrubs and fences in the open. In contrast to poison ivy *(Rhus radicans)* which is another common 3-leaved vine, virgin's-bower has *thin opposite* leaves with *prominent veins*. After the flowering period the seeds are adorned by billows of persistent silvery-gray plumes.

SH,BR,GS   2×   Crowfoot family

31

LEATHER-FLOWER *Clematis viorna*

Except for their yellowish color, the seed plumes of leather-flower closely resemble those of virgin's-bower *(Clematis virginiana)*, but the flowers of these two native vines are entirely different. In leather-flower, a scarce plant in much of the southern mountains, the purple bell-shaped flower is made up of exceptionally thick sepals that are recurved and nodding. Petals are entirely lacking. The opposite, compound leaves are 1–3½ in. long. In rich soil, this vine may climb for a distance of 10–12 ft. over shrubs and fences. It flowers from May into July.

BR,GS 2× Crowfoot family

MARSH-MARIGOLD *Caltha palustris*

Since marshes, swamps, and other wet habitats are rare over large areas in the southern mountains the more or less aquatic species of plants such as marsh-marigold and fragrant waterlily *(Nymphaea odorata)* are likewise scarce; the former does not even occur in the Great Smoky Mountains. Marsh-marigolds are succulent, with erect hollow stems 1–2 ft. high, bearing several showy bright yellow flowers. These blossoms, 1–1½ in. across with 5–9 petal-like sepals and numerous stamens, bloom from April to June. The lower leaves—round, kidney, or heart-shaped—are 2–8 in. across.

SH,BR 5× Crowfoot family

WILD COLUMBINE
Aquilegia canadensis

Columbines are wildflowers of cliffs and rocky slopes where from April to September they display beautiful scarlet and yellow blossoms. The nodding flowers have 5 petal-like sepals and 5 tubular petals that project backward between the sepals into long spurs. The generic name of this plant (*aquila,* "eagle") is said to refer to a fancied resemblance between the talons of the eagle and the spurs of the flower. The stem, 1–2 ft. high, bears rather small leaves, darker above than below. The lower and basal leaves are divided 2 or 3 times into lobed and toothed leaflets. Columbines grow from the lowest altitudes to over 5,000 ft.

SH,BR,GS   1⅓ ×   Crowfoot family

WILD MONKSHOOD
Aconitum uncinatum

At high altitudes in the Southern Appalachian Mountains the attractive deep blue or purplish flowers of wild monkshood appear from July until September. A close examination of this unusual flower makes clear the appropriateness of its name—a miniature monk's hood or "friar's cap," as it is sometimes called, about an inch long. The leaves, 3–4 in. wide, are broader than long, 3–5 lobed, and coarsely toothed. The stem, 2–4 ft. long, is slender and so weak that the plant reclines or creeps. As in all members of this genus, the roots, flowers, and seeds are poisonous. Pollination of monkshood flowers is almost entirely by bumble bees.

SH,BR,GS   ⅔ ×   Crowfoot family

33

BLACK SNAKEROOT
Cimicifuga racemosa

Attractive in appearance but disagreeable in the odor of its white flowers, black snakeroot displays its long wandlike stalk of bloom in rich woodlands from June into August. The slender stems are long (3–8 ft.) and leafy above, bearing alternate, compound leaves with coarsely toothed margins. It ranges in elevations up to 4,000 ft. This is one of several plants which the Indians regarded as helpful in case of snake bite. Other names include "black cohosh" and "bugbane," the latter from its generic name *Cimicifuga*, "to drive away bugs."

SH,BR,GS   10×   Crowfoot family

WHITE BANEBERRY
Actaea pachypoda

This plant is more showy in fruit than in flower. From late July through September it bears glossy white, oval, berrylike fruits, accounting for its alternate names of "doll's-eyes" and "white-beads." The berries are attached to the stem by thick red stalks and are reputed to be poisonous. The small white flowers (April–June) grow on short terminal stalks, and the leaves are triple compounded, with pointed, sharply toothed leaflets. This plant, usually 1–2 ft. high, is rather uncommon but does occur occasionally in rich woods at elevations up to 5,000 ft.

SH,BR,GS   4×   Crowfoot family

SHRUB-YELLOWROOT
Xanthorhiza simplicissima

In the southern mountains shrub-yellowroot, with its thin, parsleylike leaves and bright yellow roots is fairly common along low-altitude watercourses (to 2,500 ft.) and in damp woods. It is a low (1–2 ft. high), weak shrub with cleft and toothed leaflets 1–3 in. long. Occasionally it grows in a rather dense ground cover. The small, star-shaped brownish-purple flowers are in drooping clusters. Ordinarily they appear in March or April, but if the winter has been mild the flowers may unfurl in February.

BR,GS　　1×　　Crowfoot family

MAY-APPLE　　　　　　　　　　　　　　*Podophyllum peltatum*

One sure sign of spring over most of the eastern states is the appearance of colonies of may-apple "umbrellas" in rich woods and in pastures. When fully formed these paired 5–9 lobed parasols are 1–1½ ft. tall and almost a foot across. One large, waxy-white flower appears beneath this double umbrella between April and June. In the summer this is replaced by an edible yellowish lemonlike fruit 1½–2 in. long. Both the leaves and the roots of this plant are poisonous if eaten. "Mandrake" is one of its many local names. It grows at altitudes up to 3,000 ft.

SH,BR,GS　　　　　　　　　　5×　　　　　　　　　　Barberry family

UMBRELLA-LEAF *Diphylleia cymosa*

Among the great array of Southern Appalachian herbaceous plants only a few have leaves as large and distinctive as those of umbrella-leaf. They are 1–2 ft. wide on a stem 2–4 ft. high. They somewhat resemble the umbrellalike leaves of the related may-apple, but are larger. These huge leaves are smooth and very thin, deeply cleft into approximately equal halves, each half with 5–7 lobes. A cluster of many white flowers is held erect above the leaves in May and June. In summer this is followed by blue oval-shaped berries about ½ in. in diameter. This striking plant grows in wet places at altitudes above 2,500 ft.

BR,GS   3×   Barberry family

BLUE COHOSH
Caulophyllum thalictroides

The leaflets of this plant closely resemble those of meadow-rue *(Thalictrum),* giving rise to its specific name, *thalictroides.* A stem, 1–3 ft. high, grows from a thick rootstock that has certain medicinal properties. At the summit of the stem is a loose cluster of small greenish-purple flowers, each ⅓–½ in. across, appearing in rich woods during April and May. In the summer it bears erect, blue, berrylike seeds. Numerous thin leaflets make up the compound leaf. These are 1–2 in. long and whitish beneath, oval, with 3–5 rather shallow lobes. Blue cohosh grows at altitudes up to 5,000 ft.

SH,BR,GS   1⅓ ×   Barberry family

36

FRASER MAGNOLIA   *Magnolia fraseri*

In the Great Smoky Mountains, under optimum conditions, this tree reaches record proportions. One has been measured at 9 ft. 3 in. in circumference, and specimens growing to a height of 75 or 80 ft. are not unusual. It is a common tree in the cove-hardwood forests of the Southern Appalachians where it grows at altitudes up to approximately 5,200 ft. The large, thin, deciduous leaves are arranged in whorls and have 2 earlike lobes at the base. Large creamy-white flowers (3–8 in. in diameter) are displayed from April until June. In mid-summer it produces 3–4 in. conelike fruits as shown below.

BR,GS   top 2×; bottom 4×   Magnolia family

YELLOW-POPLAR   *Liriodendron tulipifera*

Tall and straight, with distinctive square-tipped leaves and handsome flowers, yellow-poplar, or "tulip tree," is one of the truly splendid forest trees of the eastern United States. In the Southern Appalachian Mountains it is common and widespread, growing from the foothills to 5,000 ft. elevation. Specimens 5 ft. in diameter are not uncommon in the Great Smokies. May is the month of peak flowering, but blossoms have been noted in early April and occasionally into June. The specific name, *tulipifera,* "tulip-bearing," is appropriate, since this tree bears great quantities of tuliplike flowers.

SH,BR,GS   2×   Magnolia family

SWEET-SHRUB   *Calycanthus floridus*

In rich woods and along watercourses this is a fairly common shrub from low altitudes up to 4,000 ft. The oval, pointed leaves, 2–5 in. long, are aromatic. The maroon flowers, made up of similar-appearing petals and sepals, have the odor of crushed strawberries when bruised. They appear in April and may continue to bloom through most of the summer. The large fig-shaped fruits have numerous glossy-brown seeds that are reputed to be poisonous.

BR,GS   2×   Calycanthus family

38

SPICEBUSH *Lindera benzoin*

Along watercourses and in rich low-altitude woods spicebush is a common to abundant shrub, occasionally growing at elevations up to 2,800 ft. Very few woody plants come into flower as early as this one, sometimes in February in the southern mountains, long before the leaves appear. The flowers are small, fragrant, and bright yellow. In late summer the oblong fruits, ⅓ in. long, become a glossy bright red. The pointed oval-shaped leaves, 2–5 in. long, give off a strong and very pleasing lemonlike odor when crushed, as do the slender twigs when bruised.

SH,BR,GS   5×   Laurel family

BLOODROOT *Sanguinaria canadensis*

In rich low-altitude (to 3,000 ft.) forests this common wildflower is a true harbinger of spring. Often it appears before the last storms of the winter. The clean white petals are short lived. The rootstock that gives this plant its name is ½–1 in. thick and up to 4 in. long, and contains a bright orange-red juice, said to have been used medicinally as a tonic and stimulant. The large single leaf is broadly heart-shaped with 5–9 prominent lobes. Among its other names are "puccoon-root" and "red Indian paint."

SH,BR,GS   4×   Poppy family

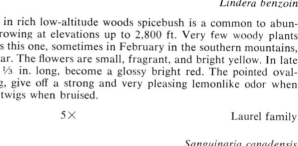

DUTCHMAN'S-BREECHES
Dicentra cucullaria

Who would mistake this well-named plant when it is in flower (April–June)–a stalk of 4–10 miniature white pantaloons, somewhat inflated, suspended in an inverted position from a slender flowering stalk? There is a touch of yellow in the area where a belt would normally girdle these little trousers. Each blossom is ½–⅔ in. long. The attractive finely divided leaves are somewhat fernlike, paler on the underside. These begin to turn yellow soon after flowering season, and by mid-summer they disappear. This little herb grows in rich woods to an elevation of at least 5,200 ft.

SH,BR,GS   1×   Poppy family

SQUIRREL-CORN   *Dicentra canadensis*

Except for its flower, this plant is much like the closely related Dutchman's-breeches. It grows in the same habitat, blossoms at the same time of year, and has almost identical finely divided leaves. On occasion these little plants are found growing side by side. But squirrel-corn has nodding flowers resembling a white bleeding heart, and this distinguishes the two species when they are in blossom. The rootstock bears numerous small tubers resembling grains of yellow corn—from which comes its common name.

BR,GS   1×   Poppy family

40

DYER'S WOAD   *Isatis tinctoria*

This Old World immigrant has been recorded only in Shenandoah National Park, where it is an abundant and conspicuous roadside plant. There its broad heads of small yellow flowers form colorful masses in the spring, to be followed in summer by attractive hanging clusters of reddish-purple seed pods. It grows 20–36 in. tall, with simple leaves. In Europe this herb was grown for an indigo dye produced from its leaves. Other dye-producing plants that have come to the eastern United States from their home in Europe include "dyer's rocket" *(Reseda luteola)* and "dyer's greenweed" *(Genista tinctoria)*.

SH   10×   Mustard family

BLACK MUSTARD   *Brassica nigra*

This common weed is a native of Europe where it is extensively cultivated for its seed, the source of our table mustard. On a stem 2–7 ft. tall appear the small showy yellow flowers, each ¼–½ in. across. They bloom throughout the summer and may continue until frost. Narrow, upright, 4-sided pods about ½ in. long soon replace the blossoms. The basal leaves have one large terminal lobe and 2–4 smaller lateral lobes all finely toothed. This widespread herb thrives in waste places and fields, occasionally becoming a troublesome weed. Cabbages, turnips, and charlocks are its close relatives.

SH,BR,GS   4×   Mustard family

CUTLEAF TOOTHWORT   *Dentaria laciniata*

In rich woods and along streambanks this is a common early spring wildflower (April and May) at low and middle altitudes. The white or pink flowers, ⅔–¾ in. wide, are arranged in a terminal stalk on a stem 8–15 in. tall. The stem leaves, usually in whorls of 3, are deeply toothed or lobed. Basal leaves ordinarily develop after the flowering season. This plant is also called "pepper-root." Other common to abundant herbs in the same family are black mustard *(Brassica nigra),* shepherd's purse *(Capsella bursa-pastoris),* whitlow-grass *(Draba* sp.), and pepper-grass *(Lepidium* sp.).

SH,BR,GS   1×   Mustard family

STONECROP   *Sedum ternatum*

"Live-forever" *(Sedum purpureum)* and "hens-and-chickens" *(Sempervivum tectorum),* so familiar in old-fashioned gardens, are European plants related to our native stonecrop. Like its European relatives, stonecrop trails over damp rocks and mossy banks. Its leaves are smooth, thick, and widened at one end. White flowers less than ½ in. across appear in April, and some may be found as late as June. The flower cluster, usually 3-forked, contains numerous leaflike bracts beneath the flowers. This plant may grow at altitudes up to 3,000 ft. in the southern mountains.

SH,BR,GS   ⅔×   Orpine family

ALLEGHENY STONECROP   *Sedum telephioides*

Like its relative stonecrop, *Sedum ternatum,* Allegheny stonecrop grows on cliffs and in rocky places. But the former is spring-blooming, whereas the latter usually blossoms during the summer. The relatively slender 6–12 in. stem holds a dense flower cluster 2–4 in. across, made up of small, pale pink, scentless flowers. Allegheny stonecrop is characterized by a delicate powdery coating of purple throughout. Other names are "wild live-forever," "cliff orpine," and "American orpine." It grows at altitudes up to 4,200 ft.

SH,BR   3×   Orpine family

MICHAUX'S SAXIFRAGE

Saxifraga michauxii
In May or June the small, white, delicate flowers of this saxifrage begin their long period of blossoming high up in the Southern Appalachian Mountains. Cliffs, rocky ledges, and mountain summits are its usual habitat. The compound cluster of little flowers grows on a 6–20 in. stem. Five white petals make up the flower. The 3 larger ones each have a pair of yellow spots at the base; the other 2 are unspotted. Each flower is ¼ in. or less across. The basal leaves grow in a rosette, are long, coarsely toothed on the margins, very hairy throughout, and a deep wine red on the underside when mature.

SH,BR,GS   2×   Saxifrage family

43

FOAMFLOWER   *Tiarella cordifolia*

A terminal stalk of delicate white flowers and a few handsome leaves that closely resemble those of red maple *(Acer rubrum)* identify this common wildflower. The upper 2–4 in. of the flowering stem (6–12 in. tall) hold the small 5-petaled blossoms April–June. The leaves, 2–4 in. long, have 3–7 lobes, with scalloped or toothed margins. The upper surface of the leaves has a loose scattering of hairs. Occasionally this plant occurs in fairly extensive colonies in rich woods and along forested roadsides, where it may grow from the lowest altitudes to over 5,000 ft.

SH,BR,GS   2×   Saxifrage family

HAIRY ALUMROOT   *Heuchera villosa*

This plant strongly resembles its relative, foamflower *(Tiarella cordifolia)*. Both have maplelike leaves of about the same size and small, delicate flowers arranged on a terminal stalk. But whereas foamflower blooms in rich woods in the spring, alumroot flowers in summer (June–September) on cliffs and rocky places. Also, alumroot grows taller (8–32 in.) with substantial hairiness on stems and undersurfaces of the leaves. Its small flowers have white to pink petals and prominently displayed stamens. It grows at middle and high altitudes. Marbled alumroot, *Heuchera pubescens,* bearing greenish flowers, is common in Shenandoah National Park.

BR,GS   3×   Saxifrage family

MITERWORT *Mitella diphylla*

So delicate and inconspicuous is miterwort, or "bishop's-cap," that it is often overlooked. Slender stems 8–18 in. tall bear 5–20 very small, white, cup-shaped flowers spaced singly along the upper 3–6 in. In addition to the long-stemmed, maplelike basal leaves, it has a pair of stemless, smaller leaves growing opposite each other near the middle of the main stem. This fairly common wildflower grows in rich rocky woods at altitudes up to approximately 3,000 ft. It flowers from late April to early June. "Fairy-cup" is another of its names.

SH,BR,GS   1×   Saxifrage family

GRASS-OF-PARNASSUS
Parnassia asarifolia

Neither the leaves nor flowers of this attractive plant resemble "grass." The smooth, bright green, basal leaves (2–3 in. wide) are rounded and broadly kidney-shaped at the base. The resemblance of these leaves to those of wild ginger (*Asarum*) is indicated by the species name. A single, round, clasping leaf grows near the middle of the stem. At the top of the 8–10 in. stem is a single, white, 5-petaled flower about 1 in. wide, its petals strongly veined with green. This plant grows in cool, wet, rocky habitats, usually at high altitudes (to 6,500 ft.), where it flowers from late July into September.

BR,GS   1×   Saxifrage family

45

WILD HYDRANGEA   *Hydrangea arborescens*

Extending from the lowest altitudes in the foothills to 6,500 ft. on some of our highest mountains, wild hydrangea is one of the most wide-ranging shrubs in the Southern Appalachians. It is a very common woody plant, occurring in various types of forests where it grows along banks of streams and on rocky slopes. It usually grows 4–10 ft. high. The thin, oval, opposite leaves are 3–6 in. long with sharply toothed margins. Along the margin of the flat-topped compound flower cluster are a few larger, showy, white sterile flowers. The peak blossoming season is in June and July, but it is not unusual to find some flowers throughout the summer months.

SH,BR,GS   1½ ×   Saxifrage family

ROUNDLEAF GOOSEBERRY   *Ribes rotundifolium*

Since this shrub does not have round leaves, both its common and scientific names are misnomers. Like most gooseberries, its leaves are lobed. Another name, "mountain gooseberry", is more appropriate, as it grows up to the summits of some of the highest peaks in the Southern Appalachians. It is a common shrub, with small slender spines and with greenish-purple flowers that appear in May and June. The smooth, round fruits, ⅓ in. in diameter, ripen in August and September.

SH,BR,GS   1½ ×   Saxifrage family

46

WITCH-HAZEL   *Hamamelis virginiana*

Witch-hazel is the only native woody plant that displays its blossoms in the autumn. It is a common, wide-ranging shrub or small tree that may reach a height of 25 ft. Small yellow flowers appear from late September to October. They consist of 4 narrow, elongated, ribbon-shaped petals ½–¾ in. long. The wavy-margined, broadly oval leaves are 2–5 in. long, short stemmed, and quite unequal at the base. There are those who believe that underground water or precious metals can be located by the proper use of a divining rod cut from the shoots of this plant. The bark and leaves are used medicinally.

SH,BR,GS   10×   Witch-hazel family

NINEBARK   *Physocarpus opulifolius*

Although this is a fairly common shrub in the higher elevations of the Blue Ridge Mountains, it is rare in the Great Smokies where it appears to be restricted to limestone ledges. This plant, 3–10 ft. tall, is characterized by the shredding bark that peels off in thin strips and gives it its name. Small, white or purplish flowers appear from May to July, arranged in a rounded terminal cluster. The 1–2 in. leaves are 3-lobed, with irregular toothed margins.

SH,BR,GS   1½ ×   Rose family

DWARF SPIRAEA   *Spiraea corymbosa*

This low shrub, ½–3 ft. tall, is relatively common along trails in Shenandoah National Park, scarce along the Blue Ridge Parkway, and absent from the Great Smoky Mountains. The broadly oval leaves are approximately 1½–3 in. long and 1–2 in. wide. They are unequally toothed especially, along their outer half, so that they resemble birch leaves *(Betula sp.)* In fact dwarf spiraea was formerly known as "birchleaf spiraea" *(S. betulifolia).* The small white or pale pink flowers are arranged in a dense terminal cluster. Dwarf spiraea grows in rocky places, where it flowers in June and July.

SH,BR   2×   Rose family

GOAT'S-BEARD   *Aruncus dioicus*

From May to July when this tall plant displays its large feathery sprays of creamy-white blossoms, it is one of the most striking wildflowers in the woodlands. The stem may be 3–6 ft. high and the stalk of small flowers 6–10 in. long. The leaves are twice or three times compound. The leaflets are long-pointed, thin, 1–3 in. long with doubly notched margins. In rich woods and forested ravines it may grow from the lower altitudes up to more than 5,000 ft. The species name, *dioicus,* indicates that it is dioecious, i.e., the male and female flowers grow on separate plants.

SH,BR,GS   4×   Rose family

BOWMAN'S-ROOT   *Gillenia trifoliata*

The white flowers of this plant, scattered on the end of the branches, may remind one of the blossoms of serviceberry *(Amelanchier),* as they are approximately the same size, shape, and color. They have 5 petals about ½ in. long, usually white; but pink petals sometimes appear. The flowering season is May to July. The 1–4 ft. stem has oval leaves arranged mostly in 3's, 1½–3 in. long, short-stalked, and sharply toothed. It grows in woods at elevations up to 4,500 ft. This herb is also called "Indian-physic" and "false ipecac," as the bark of the root was once used medicinally.

SH,BR,GS   2×   Rose family

WILD CRAB   *Malus angustifolia*

When in bloom the great profusion of showy and fragrant flowers makes this a most attractive ornamental tree. The pink or rose blossoms, about an inch broad, fade to white. March to May is the usual flowering season. The leaves are thick and a shining dark green, resembling evergreen foliage. They are 1–2 in. long, ½–¾ in. wide, and usually toothed along the edge. The fruit, about an inch in diameter, is flattened at each end, yellowish when ripe (September), hard, sour, and fragrant. This uncommon thorny little tree grows in woods and bottomlands, usually at low altitudes.

SH,BR,GS   3×   Rose family

49

AMERICAN MOUNTAIN-ASH   *Sorbus americana*

At a distance the dense clusters of white flowers on this small tree resemble those of the more familiar American elder *(Sambucus canadensis),* while its compound leaves resemble those of staghorn sumac *(Rhus typhina).* In North Carolina American mountain-ash is rare below 5,000 ft., but in Virginia it occurs at approximately 3,000 ft., and grows at altitudes up to the summits of the highest mountains. One of the largest specimens on record, approximately 20 in. in diameter, grows on Mt. Le Conte in Great Smoky Mountains National Park. The flowering season extends from early June to mid-July. By September the clusters of showy orange-red or coral fruits are mature and furnish an important food for birds.

SH,BR,GS   top 2×; bottom 4×   Rose family

ALLEGHENY SERVICEBERRY   *Amelanchier laevis*

   This handsome little tree is one of the earliest to flower. At low altitudes in the southern mountains its lovely raiment of white or creamy-white blooms appears during the latter half of March unless the weather for the preceding month is exceptionally severe. The fruits ripen in summer. They are purplish, juicy, and very sweet. A specimen fully 2 ft. in diameter (the largest on record) grows near the Appalachian Trail in Great Smoky Mountains National Park. Other names for this common tree are "sarvice," "Juneberry," and "shadbush."

SH,BR,GS   10×   Rose family

HAWTHORN   *Crataegus* spp.

   Variously referred to as "haw," or "thorn," or "hawthorn," this is a large and very difficult group of shrubs, or small trees, to differentiate from one another. They are usually spiny with irregularly lobed and strongly notched leaves. The white, 5-petaled flowers grow in terminal clusters. The little applelike fruits are round or oval and usually red or yellow when ripe. More than 1,000 native species of this plant have been identified, but many of these may be hybrids.

SH,BR,GS   1½ ×   Rose family

51

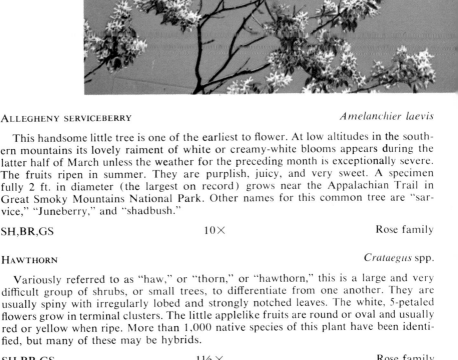

WILD STRAWBERRY   *Fragaria virginiana*

From Canada to Florida this is a very common plant in fields, on hillsides, along roadsides, and in rather dry places generally, where it propagates by means of runners. The leaves consist of 3 dark green leaflets with coarsely toothed margins, on stems 2–6 in. long. The flowers (April–June) have 5 white petals on stems about the same length as the leaf stems. The familiar and very popular red fruits, although averaging ½ in. in diameter or less, are regarded by many people as being far superior to the much larger-fruited cultivated varieties. Wild strawberry grows from the lowest altitudes to over 5,000 ft.

SH,BR,GS   top 1⅓ ×; bottom 1×   Rose family

THREE-TOOTHED CINQUEFOIL
Potentilla tridentata

This little plant with its white strawberrylike flowers grows at high altitudes in the mountains along the Blue Ridge Parkway, in Shenandoah National Park (Hawksbill Mountain), northward into Acadia National Park (Cadillac Mountain), and on to Labrador and Greenland. On stems 1–10 in. high it bears small clusters of 5-petaled flowers from June to August. The leaves, each made up of 3 leaflets, are thick, with 3 coarse teeth at the apex. It grows in dry, sterile soils and rocky crevices. It is also sometimes called "mountain five-finger" and "wineleaf cinquefoil."

SH,SR,BR   2×   Rose family

COMMON CINQUEFOIL   *Potentilla canadensis*

In old fields, along roadsides, and in waste places, at elevations up to 6,300 ft. in the southern mountains this is a common to abundant plant. Its small, yellow, 5-petaled flowers appear early in the spring—usually in March or April. The palmately-compound leaves, ½–1 in. long, have toothed margins. Common cinquefoil, also called "five-finger," spreads by means of slender runners. This plant is sometimes confused with wild strawberry *(Fragaria virginiana),* but the latter has leaflets arranged in 3's and white flowers while common cinquefoil has leaflets arranged in 5's and yellow flowers.

SH,BR,GS   1×   Rose family

53

PURPLE-FLOWERING RASPBERRY   *Rubus odoratus*

Of the many species of *Rubus* (raspberries, dewberries, and blackberries) in the Southern Appalachian Mountains, this one is unique and most easily identified. It has large, maplelike, simple leaves (in contrast to the compound leaves of all other *Rubus*). The flowers are large and rose-purple (the other species have white flowers) and the stems lack spines or prickles. This is a fairly common shrub in rich rocky soils where it grows from the lowest altitudes to 5,000 ft. Since the flowering season may begin as early as middle May and extend throughout the summer, it is not unusual to find flowers and ripe red fruits at the same time. The berries, although edible, are rather tasteless. "Thimbleberry" is another name for it.

SH,BR,GS   2×   Rose family

RASPBERRIES, DEWBERRIES, AND BLACKBERRIES   *Rubus* spp.

Plants of the genus *Rubus,* including raspberries, dewberries, and blackberries, are collectively called "brambles." Over 200 species of brambles are described in the latest (eighth, 1950) edition of *Gray's Manual of Botany,* and there is considerable difference of opinion as to how many of these are valid. Undoubtedly many of these species overlap; among the blackberries, in particular, hybridization occurs rather freely.

SH,BR,GS   1×   Rose family

CANADIAN BURNET
Sanguisorba canadensis

Since this impressive wandlike plant requires boggy soils it grows best in Big Meadows Swamp where the branched spikes, 3–8 ft. tall, display their white flowers from late July into September. Canadian burnet lacks petals, but the numerous long white filaments of the stamens are quite showy. There are 7-15 sharply toothed leaflets on the lower leaves of this plant. *Sanguisorba,* meaning "to absorb blood" refers to *S. officinalis* of Europe and Asia, which has deep red or purplish flowers and is reputed to have astringent properties. It is recorded in only a few of our states.

SH   10×   Rose family

CAROLINA ROSE   *Rosa carolina*

Wild roses are uncommon to rare in the southern mountains. Like their relatives the blackberries *(Rubus* spp.) these shrubs hybridize readily, and as a result they are hard to identify, even by the professional botanist. Carolina rose is a low (1–3 ft.) shrub which grows in open, dry, rocky or sandy places. It is also called "wild rose" and "pasture rose." The 5-petaled pink flower, 1¼–2 in. wide, mostly solitary, blooms May–June. The 5–9 leaflets are 1–3 in. long with finely toothed margins. Sharp prickles are scattered along the stems and the fruits are bright red.

SH,BR,GS   3×   Rose family

55

PIN CHERRY   *Prunus pensylvanica*

From 3,000 ft. to the summits of the highest mountains this is a common to abundant tree in areas where fire or other disturbances have removed the forest cover in recent decades. In such places pin cherry may grow in dense stands, but being short-lived it soon gives way to other species. The smooth, shining, lancelike leaves resemble those of a peach tree *(P. persica).* Clusters of small white flowers appear with the young leaves from April to early June. The small, sour, glossy-red fruits ripen in August and are sought after by various birds, bears, and other wildlife.

SH,BR,GS   2×   Rose family

CHOKECHERRY   *Prunus virginiana*

This is mostly an uncommon to rare shrub or small tree, especially in the Great Smokies where it was first recorded only in 1953. The thin, pointed leaves are oval, shorter and broader than those of the more common black cherry *(P. serotina),* and the leaf margins are finely toothed. From April to June it displays numerous small white 5-petaled flowers in elongated clusters 3–5 in. long. The drooping clusters of fruit ripen in July and August. They are glossy red or almost black—very attractive but quite astringent. Chokecherries grow along riverbanks, borders of woodlands, and in rocky places.

SH,BR,GS   5×   Rose family

56

PARTRIDGE-PEA   *Cassia fasciculata*

On open hillsides, in dry fields, along railway embankments, and in sandy soil partridge-pea attains a height of 1–3 ft. The leaves consist of 10–15 pairs of small, narrow leaflets that are somewhat delicate to the touch. The showy yellow flowers, about 1 in. across, grow 2–4 together in clusters on the stem. Of the 5 flower petals 2 or 3 often have a purple spot at the base. Flowers normally in July–September. The fruit is a straight, narrow, many-seeded pod 1½–2½ in. long, which, when mature, bursts and expels the seeds forcibly. This is a fairly common plant in some localities.

SH,BR,GS   1×   Pulse family

REDBUD   *Cercis canadensis*

In the limestone soils of the foothills, at elevations below 3,000 ft., redbud is a locally abundant little tree. At lower altitudes, in soils of high acidity its distribution is irregular and spotty. Being a very attractive and popular plant it is widely used as an ornamental. Its magenta, pealike blossoms are at their peak in late March and throughout April, often appearing before the leaves. The fruit is a many-seeded flat pod, 2–3 in. long about ½ in. wide. "Judas-tree," another name for it, may be applicable to the European relative *C. siliquastrum* but hardly to this native redbud.

SH,BR,GS   1×   Pulse family

57

YELLOWWOOD

Cladrastis lutea

In the Great Smoky Mountains where this tree grows in rich rocky soils it is uncommon and localized. Yellowwood usually occurs singly but in a few ravines branching from the Sugarlands Valley, it grows in colonies. One such place is along the Huskey Gap Trail; another, along the Big Locust Nature Trail. In bloom this is one of our most handsome native trees—a profusion of long, white, wisterialike flower clusters. If the weather in early spring has been mild, it may flower in mid-April, but ordinarily it blooms in May. The smooth blackish bark of the mature trees is distinctive. The altitudinal range of yellowwood is from 1,700 to approximately 3,600 ft.

GS 40× Pulse family

BLACK LOCUST

Robinia pseudoacacia

From the lowest altitudes to 5,300 ft. this is a common to abundant tree along riverbanks and on mountainsides where second-growth forests prevail. It usually grows tall and spindly, with girth less than 12 in. From 9 to 19 small, oval leaflets compose a leaf, and small sharp spines occur along the branches. Flowers appear from mid-April to late June. The pealike blossoms are white or cream-colored, very fragrant, and arranged in dense drooping plumes.

SH,BR,GS 2× Pulse family

58

BRISTLY LOCUST   *Robinia hispida*

This is a common shrub along the road shoulders between Roanoke and Gillespie Gap on the Blue Ridge Parkway and on dry hillsides, but elsewhere it is mostly scarce or absent. Bristly locust, 2–9 ft. high, is well named, with brownish bristles covering many parts of the plant. Loose plumes of pealike, pink or rose-purple flowers appear in May and June. Except for their hairy stems, the leaves resemble those of the more familiar black locust *(R. pseudoacacia)*. The seed pods, 2–3 in. long, are flat and bristly. It is often cultivated.

BR,GS   1½ ×   Pulse family

NAKED-FLOWERED TICK-TREFOIL
Desmodium nudiflorum

The small, roughly triangular seed pods of this common weed have hooked bristles that enable them to steal a ride of considerable distance by adhering to the clothing of people or to the hair or wool of animals. It is one of a number of "stick-tights" or "beggar-ticks" growing in the southern mountains. Ordinarily these slender-stemmed plants have small pink or purplish, pealike flowers and leaves composed of 3 leaflets. Naked-flowered tick-trefoil grows 2–3 ft. tall in fields and on dry hillsides where it blooms during the summer. The terminal cluster of flowers and the trios of leaflets are on separate stems.

SH,BR,GS   1½ ×   Pulse family

59

WOOD-VETCH   *Vicia caroliniana*

Along roadsides and riverbanks, on cliffs, and in rich woods this common little vetch grows from the lowest altitudes to 3,500 ft. The small compound leaves, each made up of 6–12 pairs of leaflets, terminate in tendrils by which this slender vine trails or climbs. If the winter has been mild, flowers may appear in March, but ordinarily the blossoming season is from April to June. There are 8–20 white, pealike flowers in a cluster, each about ⅓ in. long. The seed pods mature by late summer and are flat, pointed, approximately 1 in. long.

SH,BR,GS   2×   Pulse family

COMMON WOOD-SORREL   *Oxalis montana*

At high altitudes in the spruce-fir forests of the Blue Ridge and Great Smoky Mountains this little wood-sorrel thrives in the cool dampness of the woodland floor. Creeping by slender rhizomes, it may form large colonies of shamrocklike plants that become studded with 5-petaled, single flowers in June and July. These, ½–¾ in. wide, white with thin, deep pink veins, occur on stalks as long or longer than the leaves. Common wood-sorrel occurs in Europe, Asia, and Africa as well as in the Canadian Zone forests in eastern North America.

SH,BR,GS   ⅔×   Wood-sorrel family

60

WILD GERANIUM   *Geranium maculatum*

In rich woods over much of the eastern United States wild geranium is a common and familiar wildflower. The 5-petaled rose-purple flowers, 1–1½ in. wide, are borne on stems 1–2 ft. tall in April–June. The 3–5 lobed leaves are long stemmed if originating at the base of the plant and short stemmed (and opposite) higher up on the main stem. The long-beaked fruit accounts for another common name, "cranesbill," from the Greek *geranos,* meaning crane. The thick, horizontal root is said to have certain medicinal properties.

SH,BR,GS   2×   Geranium family

TREE-OF-HEAVEN   *Ailanthus altissima*

Although mostly scarce along the mountain tops on the Blue Ridge Parkway and in the Great Smokies, this Asiatic tree has become established in many nearby lowlands. It is an abundant weed tree in Shenandoah National Park. Spreading by basal suckers as well as by seed, tree-of-heaven usually grows rapidly. The large terminal clusters of greenish-white ill-scented flowers are displayed in June. Large, conspicuous clusters of spirally twisted 1–seeded fruit ripen in the autumn. Tree-of-heaven grows prolifically wherever it can gain a foothold.

SH,BR,GS   2½×   Quassia family

61

FRINGED POLYGALA

Polygala paucifolia

From late April through June this rare plant bears 1–5 exceptionally handsome rose-purple flowers on a stem 3–6 in. tall. These blossoms, ⅔–1 in. long, have crested and exquisitely fringed petals which superficially resemble some of the fairest of our orchids. In addition to its 3 connected petals the plant has 5 leaves at the base of the flower, 2 of which are colored like the petals. There are also a few smaller, scalelike leaves along the stem. Fringed polygala grows at elevations up to 2,500 ft. in rich woods and ravines.

SH,BR,GS   ½ ×   Milkwort family

FLOWERING SPURGE

Euphorbia corollata

In this fairly common bright green plant the small white flowers grow at the summit of a stem 1–3 ft. high. The 5 white bracts look like petals, but actually the true flowers are encircled by these bracts and are very minute. The flowering season is long: May to October. Below the flat heads of flowers the leaves are alternate and scattered, while higher up they are opposite or whorled. This rather inconspicuous herb grows in dry soil up to 4,200 ft. elevation, especially in openings in the woods or along roadsides.

SH,BR,GS   2×   Spurge family

STAGHORN SUMAC *Rhus typhina*

The branches of this shrub are so densely covered with minute hairs that they resemble the antlers of a deer in the "velvet"—giving rise to the name "staghorn." Like other sumacs, staghorn sends up numerous shoots from its roots, forming dense thickets. Although it is usually classed as a shrub, some specimens become treelike. Greenish flowers borne in dense terminal clusters are displayed from May to July. The sharply toothed leaves turn a bright red in mid-summer. Staghorn sumac is a common shrub along roadsides, on open hillsides, and elsewhere in dry rocky soil where it grows from the lowest altitudes to 5,100 ft.

SH,BR,GS 4× Cashew family

AMERICAN HOLLY *Ilex opaca*

The thick, evergreen, spiny-margined leaves and glossy red fruits of this holly symbolize the Christmas season. It is a fairly common tree in moist woods in the Great Smoky Mountains where it grows to 4,000 ft. Along the Blue Ridge Parkway it is scarce. Small, white, inconspicuous flowers are displayed in May and early June while the attractive fruits may persist throughout the winter. The hard ivory-colored wood is often used in the carving of various small animals by the Cherokee Indians.

SH,BR,GS 1½× Holly family

STRAWBERRY-BUSH   *Euonymus americanus*

Inconspicuous, small, greenish-purple flowers less than ½ in. across may appear on this shrub in mid-April if the preceding season had been mild, but ordinarily the peak of flowering is throughout May. In late summer, however, this plant comes into its glory; then the rough, crimson, 3–5-lobed capsules split open, exposing bright glossy-red (or orange) seeds. The local name "hearts a-bustin' with love" then becomes clear. This shrub is 2–8 ft. tall with 4-angled green or pale gray twigs. Its opposite bright green leaves are 1½–3 in. long. From the lowest altitudes to 3,500 ft., it grows in rich woods, ravines, and along stream courses.

SH,BR,GS   top 1⅓ ×; bottom 1×   Staff-tree family

64

RED MAPLE *Acer rubrum*

This abundant tree grows in a variety of habitats from the lowest altitudes to over 6,000 ft. It is one of the few plants occurring in all the types of forests in the southern mountains. In the Great Smokies some specimens attain a trunk diameter of over 5 ft. These large trees have a flaky or shaggy bark in contrast to the smooth gray bark on young trees. At low altitudes red maple is usually in flower before the end of February while at high elevations it may still have blossoms in early May. The flowers are reddish or yellowish—as are the leaves in October. The leaf stems are reddish.

SH,BR,GS   1×   Maple family

SPOTTED TOUCH-ME-NOT *Impatiens capensis*

Two closely related species of touch-me-nots or "snapweeds" are common in the southern mountains, this species and yellow-flowered or pale touch-me-not (*I. pallida*). Both are about 2–5 ft. tall, grow in moist ground or in water, are succulent annuals with watery juice, and have oval, coarsely-toothed leaves. Spotted touch-me-not has attractive orange flowers, mottled with reddish-brown spots, and are suspended from thread-like supports. Both plants have pods which when mature burst suddenly upon being touched. The flowering season is June–September.

SH,BR,GS   2×   Touch-me-not family

65

NEW JERSEY TEA *Ceanothus americanus*

Along roadsides, on open hillsides, and in dry sandy places, this low shrub is a common plant from the lowest altitudes to 5,400 ft. Ordinarily it does not grow taller than 3 ft. The leaves, about 1–3 in. long by ½–1½ in wide, are characterized by 3 prominent veins and finely toothed margins. Dense clusters of white flowers that have the appearance of miniature snowballs decorate New Jersey tea from mid-May to early August. Its deep, reddish root yields a brownish or cinnamon dye. During colonial times the leaves were dried and used as a substitute for tea.

SH,BR,GS   10×   Buckthorn family

MOUNTAIN STEWARTIA *Stewartia ovata*

Unfortunately, this lovely shrub is rare in the southern mountains. It has been recorded only in the Great Smokies where it occurs irregularly in a rather narrow altitudinal belt from 1,000 to 2,500 ft. The large, showy, cream-colored flowers, 2–3 in. across, are displayed in rich woods or along streambanks in June and July. These handsome solitary blossoms have 5 (rarely 6) scallop-margined petals surrounding numerous yellow or purplish stamens (the two flowers in the photograph are from different plants). "Mountain camellia," as it is sometimes called, is related to the camellias and to the tea plant of commerce.

GS   2×   Tea family

66

SPOTTED ST. JOHN'S-WORT   *Hypericum punctatum*

The height of this fairly common plant varies from 8 in. to approximately 3 ft. Small yellow flowers appear from June or July into September. They seem to crowd the top of the stem. A close examination reveals the numerous stamens that characterize this family of plants. Black spots on the petals and leaves account for its name. The 5 petals of the flower are twice the length of the 5 sepals, each blossom being approximately ½ in. across. The opposite leaves are stemless or somewhat clasping, 1–3 in. long.

SH,BR,GS   1×   St. John's-wort family

PANSY VIOLET   *Viola pedata*

Of approximately 40 to 50 species of violets in the southern mountains (32 in the Great Smokies), pansy violet has the largest flowers and is regarded by many as the most handsome. Flowers appear in April and may persist into June. The leaves have 3 main divisions, but the lateral ones are divided again into slender or widened segments, which account for the names "bird's-foot" or "crowfoot violet." While the two-colored pansy violet is relatively uncommon, a uniformly pale blue variety *(V. p. lineariloba)* is abundant in some areas.

SH,BR,GS   2×   Violet family

67

ARROW-LEAVED VIOLET   *Viola sagittata*

   Approximately three-fourths of the large variety of violets in the Southern Appalachian Mountains are blue or purplish, including arrow-leaved violet with its violet-
purple or deep blue petals. Its flower stalks are about as long as the leaf stems. Like most
other violets it blooms in middle and late spring. The leaves, 1–4 in. long, are arrow- or
spade-shaped, usually pointed at the tip, and squared or heart-shaped at the base where
prominent teeth or lobes project sideways. Closely related species of violets hybridize
readily, and this is particularly true of arrow-leaved violet.

SH,BR,GS   1⅓ ×   Violet family

ROUND-LEAVED VIOLET   *Viola rotundifolia*

   Of the relatively few yellow-flowered violets this well-named species is most readily
identified. Its round leaves, approximately an inch across at flowering time, grow to be
2–4 in. wide in the summer, and since they then become quite smooth and lie flat on the
ground their resemblance to the evergreen foliage of galax *(Galax aphylla)* is striking.
This bright yellow flower has brown veins in the 3 lower petals. It blooms so early
(March and April) that it is usually out of flower at the peak of the spring wildflower
displays (late April). It grows in rich cool woods, especially along roads and trails.

BR,GS   2×   Violet family

CANADA VIOLET   *Viola canadensis*

This leafy-stemmed white-flowered violet may attain a height of 18-20 in., making it the tallest member of this popular family of plants in our area. The leaves are broadly oval or heart-shaped with pointed tips and toothed margins. Flowers may appear by late April and continue their bloom into July or later. The lower petal is striped with fine dark lines, and there is usually a tinge of bluish or violet on the back of the upper petals. Canada violet grows in rich woods at altitudes up to 4,000 ft.

SH,BR,GS   ⅔ ×   Violet family

PASSION-FLOWER   *Passiflora incarnata*

Along roadsides, in open rocky places, and in old fields where dry conditions prevail passion-flower is a fairly common tendril-bearing vine that may climb to a height of 10 or 20 ft. Its large, showy, pale-lavendar flowers are displayed from May or June until mid-summer. These are 1½–2 in. wide, rather fantastic in the arrangement of the floral parts, and quite fragrant. The alternate, deeply 3-lobed leaves have finely toothed margins. The fruit is a many-seeded berry the size and shape of a lemon. When ripe it is yellow and edible. This fruit accounts for the alternate names "wild apricot" and "maypop."

BR,GS   1 ×   Passion-flower family

MEADOW-BEAUTY   *Rhexia virginica*

Meadow-beauty is scarce or absent throughout most of the southern mountains because its habitat is marshes and moist low-altitude meadows. Showy, purplish-pink 4-petaled flowers, 1–1½ in. wide, appear in terminal clusters July–September. Bright yellow anthers that are unusually long and curved help to identify this group of plants. The stem, 8–18 in. tall, is square and slightly winged at its angles. Stemless or short-stemmed leaves, 1–2 in. long and ½–1 in. wide, grow in opposite fashion along the stem. These are conspicuously 3–5-veined, with fine marginal teeth. Another name for this plant is "deer-grass."

BR,GS   1⅓ ×   Melastoma family

FIREWEED   *Epilobium angustifolium*

Along the northern extent of the Parkway and in Shenandoah, this tall leafy-stemmed herb is locally plentiful to abundant, particularly in areas recently devastated by fire—from which it gets its common name. The slender sharp-pointed, willowlike leaves, 2–6 in. long by ⅓–1 in. wide, account for another very appropriate name, "great willow-herb." At the summit of a stem 2–7 ft. it bears a spikelike cluster of purplish-pink or magenta flowers from July to September. The long and very slender capsules bear numerous seeds with white silky tufts.

SH,BR   12×   Evening-primrose family

70

EVENING-PRIMROSE
Oenothera biennis

In its first year evening-primrose grows in the form of a rather coarse, flattened rosette of leaves. In the second year a stout stem develops, 1–5 ft. tall, with narrow stemless leaves. With summer come bright yellow flowers. Although each blossom lasts but a day (or night), new ones continue to appear until autumn frosts. These fragrant blossoms open in late afternoon or near sunset. Each is 1–2 in. across and has 4 petals and 8 stamens. The fruiting capsules, ¾–1½ in. long, are elongated and grow erect. This common to abundant plant ranges over a large part of the United States.

SH,BR,GS   3×
Evening-primrose family

SUNDROPS   *Oenothera fruticosa*

This may be regarded as a day-blooming species of the closely related evening-primrose (*O. biennis*). It is a shorter-stemmed and altogether more slender plant, much less coarse than its wide-ranging cousin. Ordinarily the flowers of sundrops are at least as large as those of evening primrose, but they lack fragrance and are normally out of bloom before the end of summer; the fruiting capsule of sundrops is winged and less than half as long as that of its relative.

SH,BR,GS   1½×
Evening-primrose family

71

ENCHANTER'S NIGHTSHADE   *Circaea alpina*

   Enchanter's nightshade is uncommon in the southern mountains, where it grows in cool moist forests at the highest altitudes. It is a low, weak, succulent-appearing herb on a slender stem 3–8 in. high. During the summer it bears minute white flowers, each about 1/12 in. across, in a terminal cluster. Its opposite leaves, 1–2 in. long, are thin, pointed, coarsely toothed on the margins, and somewhat glossy.

SH,BR,GS   1½ ×   Evening-primrose family

WILD SARSAPARILLA   *Aralia nudicaulis*

   Both this plant and the closely related ginseng *(Panax quinquefolius)* are uncommon in the southern mountains, where they grow in rich woods. Both have been sought for their roots—that of wild sarsaparilla as a flavoring and that of ginseng as a cure-all for every ill. The flowers of both of these plants are arranged in clusters, those of sarsaparilla are in 3's while in ginseng the cluster occurs singly. Sarsaparilla fruits are purplish-black; those of ginseng, bright crimson. The greenish-white flowers of sarsaparilla are displayed in May and June while the yellowish-green blossoms of ginseng appear in July and August.

SH,BR,GS   2×   Ginseng family

SPOTTED COWBANE   *Cicuta maculata*

This poisonous plant is uncommon in the southern mountains. It looks like the related and much more plentiful wild carrot *(Daucus carota),* but is a taller, stouter plant with hollow 3–8-ft.-tall stems (except where the leaves are attached) streaked with purple, especially near the lower part of the stem. Cowbane leaves are not nearly as "ferny" as those of wild carrot. The very poisonous fleshy roots resemble small sweet potatoes and smell like parsnips. It blooms from June to September. "Water-hemlock" is another of its many names.

SH,BR,GS   3×   Parsley family

HAIRY ANGELICA   *Angelica venenosa*

Because some snakes are venomous, all kinds of snakes are feared by many people. So also with plants. Since the parsley family includes such deadly plants as poison hemlock *(Conium maculatum)* and spotted cowbane *(Cicuta maculata),* all species that resemble these to any extent become suspect. Hairy angelica is an example, and that is why it is called *venenosa,* meaning "very poisonous." Actually this angelica may have its virtues since one botanist writes that the leaves are used to discourage the use of tobacco. The dense short hairs that cover the flat flower head and upper part of the stem of this plant account for the "hairy" part of its name. It flowers from July to September.

SH,BR,GS   8×   Parsley family

73

COW-PARSNIP   *Heracleum maximum*

With stout stems 4–8 ft. high, leaves to 12 in. or more wide, and big umbrellalike heads of white flowers, cow-parsnip is one of the giants among herbaceous plants. The stem, coarse and prominently ridged, has a covering of fine silky hairs. The leaves are in 3's, the leaflets being deeply lobed with toothed margins. From 8 to 30 rays make up one of the flat-topped flower heads which bear innumerable small white flowers in June and July. Sometimes called "masterwort," cow-parsnip grows from coast to coast in moist ground, waste places, and along streambanks.

SH,BR,GS   10×   Parsley family

WILD CARROT   *Daucus carota*

Entire fields are occasionally whitened by the lacy umbrellas of this European immigrant. The small white flowers are arranged in a circular flat-topped head. Upon close examination one finds that the central flower is dark purple. When the blossoms fade the head becomes deeply concave, resembling a small bird's nest. The finely divided leaves have a somewhat feathery appearance. This plant is closly related to the common carrot, and the deep, fleshy root looks like a carrot. "Queen Anne's lace," as it is often called, flowers throughout the summer.

SH,BR,GS   5×   Parsley family

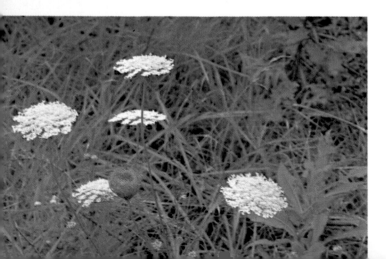

74

FLOWERING DOGWOOD   *Cornus florida*

   This is one of the most common small trees in the southern mountains where it grows in woodlands at low and middle altitudes. Above 3,000–4,000 ft. it becomes rather scarce, although specimens grow at elevations of almost 5,000 ft. in parts of the Great Smokies. What appears superficially to be a single flower is actually a dense cluster of very small greenish-white blossoms surrounded by 4 large petal-like bracts. These ordinarily reach their peak in late April, although this may take place early the following month in a late season. The opposite, oval-shaped leaves turn red in the autumn. The clusters of glossy scarlet fruits are eaten by squirrels and a variety of birds.

SH,BR,GS   top 6×; bottom 1⅓ ×   Dogwood family

SPOTTED WINTERGREEN   *Chimaphila maculata*

In dry forests where pines and oaks are the dominant trees, this little evergreen plant is common. From a trailing underground stem it sends up short branches, 4–8 in. tall, at the summit of which nodding waxy-white flowers (1–5) are produced in June and July. They are ½–¾ in. across. The opposite, leathery, dark green leaves, 1–3 in. long, are white-striped—not "spotted" as the common name indicates. A few prominent teeth are spaced rather widely around the leaf margins. Spotted wintergreen grows from the foothills to a 4,500 ft. elevation.

SH,BR,GS   2×   Wintergreen family

ROUND-LEAVED WINTERGREEN   *Pyrola rotundifolia*

Although present along many of the trails in Shenandoah National Park, round-leaved wintergreen is scarce along the Blue Ridge Parkway and absent from the Great Smokies, where its place seems to be taken by galax (*Galax aphylla*). Galax has very similar leaves—evergreen, glossy, dark green, round, and leathery. Round-leaved wintergreen grows in dry woods. In July there are a number of handsome waxy-white flowers along the 6–15-in.-tall stem. These fragrant, nodding blossoms, ½–⅔ in. wide, have 5 thick petals and a prominently projecting style.

SH,BR   4×   Wintergreen family

INDIAN-PIPE   *Monotropa uniflora*

As it is entirely lacking in chloro-
phyll, Indian-pipe is white throughout
—flower, stem, and leaves—and has
a succulent waxlike appearance. Unlike the green plants that manufacture
food from sunlight, Indian-pipe de-
rives all its nourishment from de-
cayed vegetable matter in the soil.
Occasionally in September one finds
fresh specimens that are pink or even
rose. The stem is 3–8 in. tall with
scalelike leaves. The nodding solitary
flowers have bractlike petals. After
blossoming the seed capsule turns
black and becomes erect. This un-
conventional plant grows in woodlands from the lowest altitudes to
near the summits of some of the highest mountains in the eastern United
States (6,300 ft.). The flowering period begins in June, and specimens
may be found throughout the summer. It is also called "ghost flower"
and "corpse plant."

SH,BR,GS   1½ ×
Wintergreen family

ROSEBAY RHODODENDRON   *Rhododendron maximum*

Along the Blue Ridge Parkway and into the Great Smoky Mountains this large evergreen shrub is common and widespread, occurring in almost all types of forests. In
ravines and hollows and along shaded watercourses it often grows so luxuriantly as to
form almost impenetrable tangles. The peak of blossoming usually occurs in June at
the lower altitudes and July in the higher reaches (3,000–5,000 ft.). The flower buds
are a deep rose. The dark green, leathery leaves react to subfreezing temperatures by
bending downward and rolling into a tight coil.

SH,BR,GS   3 ×   Heath family

77

CATAWBA RHODODENDRON   *Rhododendron catawbiense*

When in bloom, the handsome catawba rhododendron is the most spectacular of the evergreen-leaved rhododendrons in the southern mountains. In contrast to rosebay, or great white species, catawba grows mostly from approximately 3,000 ft. upwards to the summits of the southern mountains where it thrives best on ridge-tops and open slopes away from the shade of the forest. It may grow as low as 1,000 ft. in the mountains of northern Virginia. June is its flowering month.

SH,BR,GS   5×   Heath family

FLAME AZALEA   *Rhododendron calendulaceum*

Since the time of William Bartram this spectacular plant, "the most gay and brilliant flowering shrub yet known," has been a great favorite. It grows at the lowest altitudes up to 5,800 ft., especially in fairly dry open forests where pines and oaks predominate. Ordinarily the flowering period begins in late April at the lower elevations and progresses upward until late June, when the plants in the higher mountains come into full bloom. The flowers range from pale yellow to a striking rich orange, since flame azalea hybridizes readily with other species. While many specimens grow 5–8 ft. tall, some attain a height of 18 ft. in the Great Smokies.

SH,BR,GS   2×   Heath family

PINXTER-FLOWER   *Rhododendron nudiflorum*

This pink-flowered azalea may begin blooming in March, but usually these attractive honeysucklelike clusters of flowers first appear in April. They open their faintly fragrant blossoms before the leaves are unfurled, 5 stamens projecting well beyond the 2-in. wide flower. The thin leaves 2–4 in. long, are narrowly oblong and pointed at both ends. In areas away from the mountains it is usually found in swamps. It is also called "wild honeysuckle" and "swamp honeysuckle."

SH,BR,GS   10×   Heath family

MINNIE-BUSH   *Menziesia pilosa*

The leaves of this low shrub resemble those of an azalea, while the little bell-shaped flowers are much like those of the blueberry. Actually minnie-bush is related to both plant. On the northern Blue Ridge and in Shenandoah it grows at elevations over 3,000 ft., but in North Carolina and Tennessee it grows mostly in the spruce-fir forests above 5,000 ft. Its terminal flower clusters, opening in June and July, may be cream-colored or greenish-white tinged with purple. The nodding flowers are less than ¼ in. long. The oval whitish-tipped leaves, 1–2 in. long, have fine hairs along the margin, and are paler beneath.

SH,BR,GS   1×   Heath family

79

HUGER'S SAND-MYRTLE   *Leiophyllum buxifolium* var. *hugeri*

As the species name indicates, this dense, low-growing, evergreen shrub has leaves like boxwood *(Buxus)*. The small, thick leaves, ¼–½ in. long, are glossy dark green above. Huger's sand-myrtle is a plant of middle and high altitudes where it grows on rocky ridges and summits and in the heath "balds" along with mountain laurel *(Kalmia latifolia)* rhododendrons *(R. catawbiense* and *R. minus)*, and blueberries *(Vaccinium* spp.). The minute, 5-petaled white or pinkish flowers may appear by mid-April if the winter has been mild but blossoming usually takes place in May and June.

BR,GS   2×   Heath family

MOUNTAIN-LAUREL   *Kalmia latifolia*

Wherever the soil is sufficiently acid, this large evergreen shrub is common to abundant, occurring in all types of forests except the spruce-fir. It grows at the lowest altitudes up to 5,800 ft. (Great Smokies). Usually the attractive pink or white saucer-shaped flowers are so abundant that the mountain-laurel in full bloom is one of our most spectacular plants. It flowers in May and June, the later blooms ordinarily occurring on plants growing in the higher altitudes. "Ivy" and "callico-bush" are among its other names. Treelike specimens of record size grow in the Great Smoky Mountains.

SH,BR,GS   2×   Heath family

MALEBERRY   *Lyonia ligustrina*

The small white globular flowers of this uncommon deciduous shrub resemble those of dog-hobble *(Leucothë fontanesiana)* and sourwood *(Oxydendrum arboreum)*—all in the same family. These blossoms appear in late May at lower altitudes, with some flowers as late as in mid-July on plants near the summits of some of the highest eastern mountains (6,500 ft.). The oblong to oval leaves are pointed at both ends and usually bear fine teeth along the margins. They are reputed to be poisonous to young livestock. This shrub grows in open pine and oak forests and on a number of the grass balds in the Southern Appalachians.

SH,BR,GS   1½ ×   Heath family

DOG-HOBBLE *Leucothoë fontanesiana*

This weak-stemmed arching shrub grows so densely in moist, acid soils and along shaded streamsides that it forms almost impenetrable tangles. In such places it undoubtedly would impede a dog's passage through it. Dog-hobble, 3–6 ft. high, has evergreen, glossy, leathery leaves that are willowlike in size and shape and are sharply toothed along the margin. They are said to be poisonous to livestock. The small creamy-white cylindrical blossoms are displayed in drooping many-flowered clusters from late April to early June. It ranges from the lowest elevations up to 5,800 ft.

BR,GS   1 ×   Heath family

SOURWOOD   *Oxydendrum arboreum*

In the low and middle altitudes of the Blue Ridge Parkway and the Great Smoky Mountains sourwood is a common to abundant small tree, but is rare in Shenandoah National Park. In the Great Smokies it grows at elevations up to 5,600 ft. and reaches record size. When the cream-colored flowers bloom, late June to early August, they attract large numbers of bees. The numerous flowers are arranged in very attractive one-sided terminal clusters. The smooth leaves account for much of the brilliant scarlet coloration along the roadside in autumn.

SH,BR,GS   1½ ×   Heath family

TRAILING ARBUTUS   *Epigaea repens*

Over a large part of its extensive range trailing arbutus, or "mayflower," has become scarce or has disappeared, but in remote areas and in places where it is protected this prostrate shrub continues to thrive. In low- and middle-altitude forests where pines and oaks predominate this dwarf evergreen may form extensive patches. Before the last of the winter storms; the fragrant white or pink flowers, often concealed by the thick low-growing leaves, may appear. In the Great Smokies where it grows at elevations up to 5,800 ft. (Andrews Bald), it flowers until middle or late May.

SH,BR,GS   1×   Heath family

82

TEABERRY   *Gaultheria procumbens*

Like its relative trailing arbutus *(Epigaea repens),* teaberry is a dwarf creeping evergreen shrub that grows best in rather dry, acid soils, particularly in pine and oak forests.
The two plants often grow in close proximity. The small urn-shaped flowers, white or
pinkish, resemble the blossoms of the related blueberries, and may be found from June
to August. Late in autumn the conspicuous round, red, berrylike fruits ripen. They
have a spicy flavor. The dark, glossy leaves have a distinctive wintergreen flavor. Teaberry, often called "wintergreen" or "checkerberry," is an old-time remedy, used as a
diuretic.

SH,BR,GS   top 1½×; bottom 1½×   Heath family

BLUEBERRY — — — — — — — — *Vaccinium* spp.

The genus *Vaccinium* is one of the groups of plants that are "difficult" to separate both for the layman and the professional botanist. Hybridization is rather frequent, and local populations are sometimes built up around one set of characters. Considerable confusion is inevitable as in some other genera such as *Rubus* (blackberries and their relatives), *Crataegus* (hawthorns), and *Solidago* (goldenrods). Most of the so-called blueberries are low to medium-sized shrubs having rather small, thick leaves, small, white, urn-shaped flowers, and small, round, many-seeded fruits that are bluish when ripe. The fruits are an important food for bears and other forms of wildlife.

SH,BR,GS — — 2× — — Heath family

DEERBERRY — — — — — — — — *Vaccinium stamineum*

The flowers and fruits of this shrub are so different from the ordinary run of so-called blueberries that some botanists place the deerberry in another genus *(Polycodium)*. So numerous are the clusters of white or yellowish-green flowers that it is quite handsome when in bloom (April–June). The clustered stamens extend far out from the open bell-shaped flower. The round, thick-skinned berries, ¼–⅜ in. in diameter, drop to the ground soon after they ripen. A high-quality jam is made from the juicy sour berries. Locally this plant is called "squawberry" and "gooseberry."

SH,BR,GS — — — — — — 1× — — — — — — Heath family

84

BEETLEWEED   *Galax aphylla*

Along the Blue Ridge Parkway and southward into the Great Smokies this evergreen herb is common in dry open forests where the soil is sufficiently acid. There it usually occurs in extensive patches, the lustrous bright green foliage presenting an impressive spectacle. These shining circular leaves have a leathery texture, and in areas where they are not protected large quantities are gathered for the florist trade. In the autumn their green hue changes to very pleasing shades of maroon and wine. The slender spikelike clusters of small white flowers are conspicuous in May and June on a stem 1–2 ft. tall. *Galax* presumably comes from the Greek *gala,* meaning milk, in reference to the color of the flowers.

BR,GS   5×   Diapensia family

WHORLED LOOSESTRIFE
Lysimachia quadrifolia

Whorls of 4 or 5 willowlike leaves spaced at regular intervals along a stem 1–3 ft. tall are characteristic of this loosestrife. These leaves, 1–4 in. long and ¼–1 in. wide, have small black dots. Small, star-shaped, yellow flowers appear in June and July, mounted on threadlike stems arising from the leafwhorls. The number of flowers ordinarily corresponds to the number of leaves. The blossoms usually have reddish spots or streaks. Whorled loosestrife grows along roadsides and riverbottoms and in open woods at low and middle altitudes.

SH,BR,GS   2×   Primrose family

85

MOUNTAIN SILVERBELL *Halesia carolina* var. *monticola*

While silverbell is a very common tree in the Great Smoky Mountains it occurs only near the southern end of the Blue Ridge Parkway. In the Smokies it grows in all types of forests except those which are most dry (open oak and pine stands) and those which are coldest and wettest (spruce-fir). In April and May, when its new leaves begin to appear, the attractive white bell-shaped flowers appear, arranged singly and in small clusters along the branches. Trees with pink flowers occur uncommonly. It is ordinarily a small tree, but in the Smokies specimens over 2 ft. in diameter are not unusual.

BR,GS   2×   Storax family

FRINGE-TREE *Chionanthus virginicus*

When in blossom, this uncommon to rare shrub, or small tree, is quite handsome. Large, drooping sprays of slender white petals decorate the fringe-tree in May–June. It is, of course, a favorite garden ornamental and grows well in cultivation outside its natural range. The oval leaves are rather large—3–6 in. long. One-seeded fruits resembling small plums become bluish-purple when ripe. The bark of the roots is used medicinally. This plant grows along river banks, in moist woods, and on open rock outcrops at up to 3,000 ft. elevations.

SH,BR,GS   3×   Olive family

INDIAN-PINK   *Spigelia marilandica*

There is no record of this perennial herb in Shenandoah National Park or along the Blue Ridge Parkway, and in the Great Smokies it is rather scarce. There, in rich woods and damp clearings, it displays its attractive flowers at low altitudes in May and June. The 4-angled stem of this plant, 1–2 ft. tall, has opposite leaves measuring approximately 2–4 in. long and ½–2 in. wide. The tubular flower, 1–2 in. long, is scarlet on the outside and yellow within. It is also called "pink-root," "star-bloom," and "worm-grass"—the last a reference to the use of the root by pioneers for expelling or destroying intestinal worms.

GS   1×   Logania family

ROSE-PINK   *Sabatia angularis*

The species name *angularis* refers to the 4-angled stem of this attractive plant. This stem is slender and 1–3 ft. high. The opposite, clasping leaves are ¾–1½ in. long. Ordinarily the flowers are a handsome rose-pink (hence its common name), but on rare occasions white blossoms may also be found. The flowers are 1–1½ in. wide. Rose-pink grows in rather sterile soil in open woods, fields, and clearings. Other names for it are "American centaury" and "bitter-bloom"—the latter from its medicinal use as a bitter tonic.

BR,GS   2×   Gentian family

STIFF GENTIAN *Gentiana quinquefolia*

Of the various gentians in the southern mountains this species is readily recognized by the small size of the individual flowers and by the profusion of blossoms on a single plant. As many as 50 or more blooms, grouped in clusters of 2–7, may be held on a branched 4-winged stem. The tubular flowers, less than an inch long, are blue, violet, or lilac. This plant is fairly common at high latitudes (to 6,300 ft.) where its blossoms may be found from late August until frost. The opposite leaves are partly clasping. It grows in rich woods, in damp fields, and along roadsides. Such local names as "ague-weed" and "gall-weed" relate to its former use as a tonic.

SH,BR,GS   2×   Gentian family

BLUE-DOGBANE
Amsonia tabernaemontana

There are no records of this plant in Shenandoah National Park, and it is scarce to rare in the mountains to the south. Its blue flowers are displayed from April to July in rich woods and moist soil. The short funnel of the blossom expands into 5 segments resulting in a star-shaped flower. The sharp-pointed leaves, 2–4 in. long and ½–2 in. wide, are arranged alternately along a stem 2–4 ft. high. The paired erect seed pods, 3–4 in. long, are smooth and very slender.

BR,GS   2×   Dogbane family

88

COMMON PERIWINKLE   *Vinca minor*

Europe is the homeland of this hardy little evergreen vine that persists for decades around old homesites, in gardens, and cemeteries. The latter habitat has given it another local name, "graveyard grass." It has escaped from cultivation into the woods and along roadsides, where it forms an attractive ground cover. The leaves are opposite, dark green, and shining. Solitary blue or violet-blue flowers, approximately an inch across, appear like so many stars from March to July. Common periwinkle is also called "running myrtle" and "blue myrtle."

SH,BR,GS   1⅓ ×   Dogbane family

SPREADING DOGBANE   *Apocynum androsaemifolium*

Like the milkweeds *(Asclepias)*, this slender branching herb has a sticky, milky juice throughout. The stem, 1–4 ft. tall, is red on one side. The oval leaves, 2–4 in. long, have very short stems and are paler beneath. From June to August the fragrant pink or rose flowers are displayed in loose terminal clusters. The waxlike, bell-shaped flower with its 5 recurved lobes is quite handsome. The fruit is a paired slender pod approximately 4 in. long. Spreading dogbane grows in dry soils along fencerows and in fields. Its roots were once used as a tonic or laxative.

SH,BR,GS   2×   Dogbane family

Butterfly-weed   *Asclepias tuberosa*

Along roadsides and in dry fields where its flat-topped cluster of bright orange flowers receives the benefit of the hot summer sunshine, butterfly-weed is a common plant in the lower altitudes throughout the area. Not many of the native wildflowers are as conspicuous or as radiant as this one, and it appears to have a particular attraction for butterflies. Yet in many localities, where it is known as "chigger-weed," people have an unfounded prejudice against it. This handsome plant has a stout, hairy, leafy stem 1–2 ft. tall. The numerous orange or yellow flowers may be found throughout much of the summer.

SH,BR,GS   8×   Milkweed family

Four-leaved milkweed   *Asclepias quadrifolia*

The middle leaves of this milkweed are arranged in whorls of 4, but the upper and lower leaves are smaller and occur in pairs. Thus the name "four-leaved" applies only in part. The stem is slender, 1–2 ft. high, and the plant has a more delicate appearance than the other species of milkweeds. It also normally comes into bloom earlier than its relatives. The flowers, displayed from May to early summer, are white or pink and are grouped in 1 to 4 terminal clusters. The fruit is a seed pod 3–5 in. long.

SH,BR,GS   2×   Milkweed family

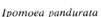

TALL MILKWEED   *Asclepias exaltata*

Often towering above the plants with which it associates, on a stem 3–6 ft. tall, this well-named milkweed has few to several loose clusters of drooping flowers which appear from June to August. The segments of the flower are pale purplish-green while the crown is ivory-white or pink. The large, thin, opposite leaves (4–9 in. long) are paler beneath. The seed pods have an unusually long point. Tall **milkweed** is abundant in Shenandoah National Park but less plentiful in the mountains to the south. It grows at elevations up to 5,500 ft. in rich woods.

SH,BR,GS   1⅓ ×   Milkweed family

WILD POTATO-VINE   *Ipomoea pandurata*

Handsome, trumpet-shaped flowers and an enormous root characterize wild potato-vine. This wild morning glory has white, funnel-shaped flowers with a lavender or crimson throat. These blossoms, 1 to 5 per plant, are 2–3 in. long. The blooming season may extend from May to September. A twining or trailing stem, 2–12 ft. long, bears heart-shaped and, occasionally, fiddle-shaped leaves 2–6 in. long. The extremely large root, weighing up to several pounds, is fleshy and contains a milky juice. Some of the North American Indians are reported to have roasted the roots in times of famine.

SH,BR,GS   5×   Convolvulus family

91

LOW BINDWEED
Convolvulus spithamaeus

Unlike other bindweeds, this morning glory has a 6–20 in. stem that ordinarily does not twine. The alternate leaves, variously described as oblong-oval, fiddle-shaped, and arrowhead-shaped, are 1–3 in. long and approximately half as wide. White, flaring, trumpet-shaped flowers, 2–2½ in. across and very showy, appear from June to August. Low bindweed grows in rocky fields and dry sandy areas in the mountainous regions.

SH,BR　2×　Convolvulus family

DODDER　　　　　　　　　　　　　　　　　　*Cuscuta compacta*

All the various species of dodders are often considered noxious, parasitic weeds. Their seeds germinate in the soil, and the young plants attach themselves to nearby herbs or shrubs by numerous small suckers. The host plant then furnishes all the food needed by the threadlike twining parasite, and its roots and lower portion soon dry up. "Lovevine" and "strangle-weed" are other names applied to this leafless, leechlike plant. Very small white flowers appear in dense clusters from July to September. Bottomlands, swamps, and streamsides are habitats where the dodder thrives.

BR,GS　　　　　　　　　　　　⅔ ×　　　　　　　　　　Convolvulus family

PHLOX

Phlox spp.

Some 40 to 50 species of phlox are listed for North America. Most of them are perennials with smooth-edged leaves arranged oppositely along the stem, and showy flowers in terminal clusters. Many species are extensively cultivated producing a great variety of forms with a wide range of colors. Most of the garden forms of perennial phlox derive from "fall phlox" *(P. paniculata)* or its hybrids. This tall-growing plant, 2–6 ft. high, is common in Shenandoah National Park and the mountains to the south, where it often escapes from gardens at old homesites. It is the only one of the 10–12 species of phlox in these mountains that may continue to bloom until frost.

SH,BR,GS 2× Polemonium family

MOSS-PHLOX

Phlox subulata

A welcome sight in early spring is the dense evergreen carpet of this low, matted phlox, studded so profusely with masses of bloom that the foliage is obscured by the flowers. The small, 5-lobed blossoms are pink, purple, or white with a darker-colored eye. It is also called "moss-pink" and "flowering moss," but it is not a moss. Moss-phlox grows at elevations up to 3,500 ft. in dry, sandy, or rocky soils. It is uncommon to rare in the southern mountains except where it has escaped from cultivation.

SH,BR,GS   10×   Polemonium family

93

WATERLEAF   *Hydrophyllum virginianum*

The white or violet flowers of waterleaf may be expected from late spring into early summer in rich moist woods. Arranged in loose drooping clusters, the individual 5-lobed blossoms are bell-shaped and about ⅓ in. long. Extending well out from the flowers are 5 very prominent stamens. The stem is slender, weak, and 1–3 ft. tall. The leaves are divided into 5–7 pointed and coarsely toothed segments. This fairly common plant grows at altitudes up to 5,000 ft.

SH,BR,GS   1×   Waterleaf family

FRINGED PHACELIA   *Phacelia fimbriata*

So abundant is this handsome little plant in the Great Smoky Mountains that extensive areas of the forest floor become whitened with the innumerable flowers in April and May. Although usually white, the flower may be tinged with pale lavender or lilac. The lobes of the cup-shaped blossoms, ⅓–½ in. across, are strongly fringed; under low magnification this flower is quite attractive. It grows on a weak stem only a few inches tall. The leaves are divided into 5–9 unequal segments—the ones above being stemless, while the lower ones are on slender stems. This plant grows at elevations from 2,500 to 5,200 ft.

BR,GS   1×   Waterleaf family

94

LOOSE-FLOWERED PHACELIA   *Phacelia bipinnatifida*

The numerous blue or violet-blue flowers of this phacelia are displayed on a branching hairy stem 1–2 ft. high. The loosely clustered blossoms, approximately ½ in. across, are bell-shaped, with prominent, long-projecting stamens. Three to 7 segments are variously lobed and coarsely toothed to make up the sharp-pointed leaves. This is a common wildflower in the Great Smoky Mountains, but it is scarce or absent in the highlands to the north. It grows at elevations up to 4,000 ft. along streamsides and in fairly damp places, where it blooms from April to June.

BR,GS   10×   Waterleaf family

VIPER'S BUGLOSS   *Echium vulgare*

The seed of this European plant is supposed to resemble the head of a poisonous serpent (viper). According to the ancient doctrine of signatures the bite of a venomous snake could be cured by the use of this plant. It is an immigrant, 1–3 ft. high, with a very bristly array of hairs covering its stem and leaves. The wavy-margined leaves are stemless except for those at the base, and become progressively smaller in ascending the stem. Showy, bright-blue flowers appear from mid-June until frost. They are pink in the bud, becoming reddish-purple when old. Viper's bugloss, also called "blueweed" and "blue-devil," grows in poor soil and dry, waste places, especially along roadsides.

SH,BR,GS   2×   Borage family

95

CORN-GROMWELL   *Lithospermum arvense*

   This is one of several European plants regarded as noxious weeds in our country. Its hard, stonelike nutlets, often found in unclean seeds of small grains and clover, retain their vitality for many years. The entire plant, 6–20 in. high, is covered with fine hairs. Its alternate bright green leaves, stemless and very narrow, are ½–1½ in. long. The small white funnel-shaped flowers, about ¼ in. long, occur in the spikes or at the base of the upper leaves. These appear in May, and some flowers may be found until mid-summer. It is a plant of dry fields and waste places.

SH,BR,GS   1⅓ ×   Borage family

SHOWY SKULLCAP *Scutellaria serrata*

   Of the dozen or more species of skullcaps *(Scutellaria),* a genus of mints, this usually has the largest flower and is recognized as the most handsome. The slender stem, simple or branched, is 1–2 ft. tall and has 4–6 pairs of oval or elliptical leaves that are coarsely toothed. The uppermost leaves are reduced to small bracts at the base of the blue flowers. The blossoms appear in late spring but, unlike many kinds of mints, are scentless. The showy flowers, each about an inch long, have tubular, curved, two-lipped flowers, with the upper arching lip shorter than the lower. Showy skullcap grows in woodlands at altitudes up to 3,000 ft.

SH,BR   1½ ×   Mint family

96

PURPLE GIANT HYSSOP
Agastache scrophulariaefolia

This tall stout mint (2–6 ft.) is fairly common, especially along the Skyline Drive in Shenandoah National Park where it may be found in attractive colonies. It is a strongly scented perennial herb with a square stem and opposite leaves, the undersides of which are covered with minute hairs. These leaves, 2–6 inches long, are coarsely toothed and conspicuously veined. The small pale-pink or purplish flowers are crowded into a dense terminal cluster that may be 3–18 inches long. Purple giant hyssop grows in rich woods and along roadsides where it flowers from late July until September.

SH,BR,GS   6×   Mint family

HEAL-ALL   *Prunella vulgaris*

This common and very widespread mint is thought to have been a native plant but has also been naturalized from Europe and Asia. In Europe, old-time herb doctors used it in the treatment of throat ailments and other afflictions, whereby it acquired its common name and such other names as "self-heal," and "carpenter's-herb." Its terminal spikes of blue or purplish flowers are held on a square stem 3–24 in. high, and may be found from May to October. Like the other mints, it has opposite leaves. Heal-all grows along roadsides and in fields and waste places.

SH,BR,GS   1×   Mint family

FALSE DRAGONHEAD
Physostegia virginiana

Swamps, riverbanks, and other wet places are the habitats of this uncommon mint. Handsome rose-pink flowers, arranged in dense terminal spikes, grow on a square stem 1–4 ft. tall during the summer. The tendency for the funnel-like flower to remain in whatever position it is placed accounts for the name "obedient plant." The opposite leaves are sharp-pointed and have sharply toothed margins. In some areas false dragonhead occurs as an escape from cultivation.

BR,GS,SH   1×   Mint family

CLINGMAN'S HEDGE-NETTLE
Stachys clingmanii

This high-altitude mint is named in honor of General Thomas L. Clingman, soldier, statesman, and scientist of North Carolina whose fame is also perpetuated in the naming of Clingmans Dome in the Great Smoky Mountains and Clingmans Peak in the Black Mountain Range of the Blue Ridge. Clingman's hedge-nettle, characterized by its covering of short hairs, is a bright green herb 20–40 in. tall. Like so many other mints it has a square stem, opposite leaves, and lipped flowers. The purple blossoms, approximately ½ in. long, are displayed in June and July.

BR,GS   1×   Mint family

LYRE-LEAVED SAGE   *Salvia lyrata*

The lyre-shaped leaves of this plant grow mostly in a basal rosette. A square stem 1–2 ft. high bears several whorls of large bluish-purple flowers from May to July. The flower, about 1 in. long, is 2-lipped, the upper part being much smaller than the lower. Lyre-leaved sage may form extensive colonies in meadows and waste places at the lower altitudes. A mint, it is related to such aromatic herbs as catnip, thyme, hoarhound, peppermint, and lavender.

SH,BR,GS   5×   Mint family

OSWEGO-TEA   *Monarda didyma*

Few of our wildflowers are as showy as the brilliantly colored Oswego-tea or "bee-balm." The vivid scarlet of these summertime blooms recalls the radiant hues of fire-pink *(Silene virginica)* and cardinal-flower *(Lobelia cardinalis)*. This very aromatic herb has a square stem 2–3 ft. tall, topped by rounded cluster of bright red flowers (July–September). These are great favorites with the ruby-throated hummingbird. Oswego-tea grows along streams and in wet soils to an elevation of 6,500 ft. It is a common plant in most of our eastern mountains, except for the Virginia Blue Ridge.

SH,BR,GS   2×   Mint family

WILD BERGAMOT   *Monarda fistulosa*

Wild bergamot closely resembles its near relative, Oswego-tea *(M. didyma)*. Both are aromatic mints of approximately the same size and general appearance, but whereas the latter has bright red flowers, blossoms of wild bergamot may be pale lilac, pale purple, or a yellowish-pink. Also the leaves of wild bergamot are narrower and more willowlike, and it grows in much drier places. Like its more brilliantly colored cousin, wild bergamot is a very aromatic herb which flowers from June to September. This plant was brewed into a tea, serving as a nerve and stomach tonic.

SH,BR,GS   2×   Mint family

MOUNTAIN-MINT
Pycnanthemum spp.

There are a number of species of these pungent aromatic herbs in our eastern mountains. Usually 1–3 ft. tall, they have the square stem, opposite leaves, and lipped flowers that are a trade-mark of the mints. In addition, this genus is often characterized by the whitish coloration.of the upper leaves and bracts, appearing as though some white powder had been dusted upon the top of the plant. The small, purple-dotted, whitish flowers are arranged in dense rounded heads. Also called "horse-mint" and "basil," mountain-mint flowers on hillsides and in fields from July to October. Various species of mountain-mint were used by the mountain people as a relief for colic, to induce perspiration, as an antispasmodic, and to distill mint oil for flavoring.

SH,BR,GS   1×   Mint family

100

HORSE-NETTLE   *Solanum carolinense*

Both this plant and hairy ground-cherry *(Physalis pubescens)* are in the same family as the cultivated potato, tomato, eggplant, red pepper, and tobacco. This family of largely tropical species also includes some very poisonous plants such as the Jimsonweeds and nightshades. Horse-nettle is readily identified by the numerous yellow prickles on its stems and leaves and by the handsome star-shaped purple (or violet) flowers. In the centers, bright orange anthers form a cone. It often grows in waste places where it flowers from May to September.

SH,BR,GS   1×   Nightshade family

HAIRY GROUND-CHERRY
        Physalis pubescens

This weak-stemmed plant is closely related to horse-nettle *(Solanum carolinense),* and it produces its flowers and fruits at about the same time of year. But it is easy to distinguish between these two nightshades. Hairy ground-cherry lacks the very prominent spines, its leaves are without lobes, and the smaller bell-shaped flowers are yellow, with dark purplish anthers at their center. It is most readily identified by a yellow, pulpy berry enclosed within a bladderlike structure resembling a miniature Japanese lantern. Flowers are present during most of the summer. This plant is often found in clearings and disturbed areas.

SH,GS   1×   Nightshade family

101

COMMON MULLEIN
Verbascum thapsus

Like many of our common "weeds," this familiar plant is of European origin. It frequents roadsides, fields, and waste places, and is a pioneer invader of recently cleared areas. On occasion it becomes a troublesome weed. Of its many local names, ones like "flannel-leaf," "velvet-plant," and "feltwort" refer to its exceptionally dense wooliness. The plant produces a rosette of basal leaves during the first year, and a tall 2–6 ft. flowering stem appears in the second year. Only a few of the yellow 5-lobed flowers appear at one time, but the blooming season may extend throughout the summer. Mullein was an old-time remedy for coughs.

SH,BR,GS   10×   Figwort family

BUTTER-AND-EGGS   *Linaria vulgaris*

The yellow and orange flowers of butter-and-eggs strongly resemble the blossoms of the closely related snapdragons. In both plants the mouth of the 2-lipped flowers will open when one's fingers apply light pressure against the sides of the tubular flower. The leaves are numerous, very narrow, and pointed at both ends. There is a protruding spur at the base of the yellow flower. Butter-and-eggs is a native of Europe and Asia. In Germany the flowers were used in making yellow dyes. This attractive plant grows along roadsides and in waste places, where it flowers from June to September.

SH,BR,GS   2×   Figwort family

White Turtlehead *Chelone glabra*

As the name indicates, these flowers closely resemble the head of a turtle. In some areas it is also called "snake-head," "cod-head," and "fish mouth." The inflated 2-lipped flowers are crowded into a dense terminal spike, and are usually white, although some are tinged with pink. They blossom July–September. Opposite willowlike leaves with sharply toothed margins grow on slender, squarish stems 1–3 ft. tall. These are dark, shining green, with prominent veins. White turtlehead is a fairly common plant of streamsides, ditches, and swamps where it may grow at elevations up to 5,500 ft. An ointment made of the leaves is reported to relieve itching.

SH,BR,GS   2×   Figwort family

Pink Turtlehead   *Chelone lyoni*

This turtlehead has handsome rose-pink flowers. In contrast to its white-flowered relative *(C. glabra)* the leaves are not as narrow, and it is more likely to occur at higher altitudes (to 6,600 ft.). Also, the pink species tends to be shorter than the white. It grows most commonly in the spruce-fir forests of western North Carolina and Tennessee, where the heavy rainfall produces a suitable habitat. The flowers are about the same size as those of white turtlehead (approximately 1 in. long) and are displayed at the same time of year (summer).

BR,GS   2×   Figwort family

BEARD-TONGUE
Penstemon canescens

In rather dry, sandy, or rocky areas the attractive flowers of beard-tongue are displayed from May to July. The plant, usually 1–2 ft. high, has a stem covered with short hairs. The opposite leaves vary in size and shape—the basal ones may be 3–6 in. long and are narrowed into long leaf stems, while the upper ones are much smaller and clasp the stem. Color of the tubular 2-lipped flowers may range from lavender to violet to pale purple or magenta, with lines of deeper hue in the throat. Only 4 of the 5 stamens are fertile; the fifth is sterile and bearded.

SH,BR,GS   4×   Figwort family

PRINCESS-TREE
Paulownia tomentosa

This Asiatic tree has escaped from cultivation and may be found growing wild from New York to Florida. In our eastern and southern mountains it grows chiefly along streams at the lower altitudes, sometimes abundantly. Except for the color of the flowers and the appearance of the seed pods this tree resembles catalpa. The large, handsome, violet flowers are displayed in April and May, before the leaves appear. The leaves are large and heart-shaped. Also called "empress-tree" and "royal Paulownia," it was named in honor of Anna Paulowna (1795–1865), princess of the Netherlands.

SH,BR,GS   8×   Figwort family

COMMON SPEEDWELL
Veronica officinalis

In commenting upon the plants he saw in the British Isles, naturalist John Burroughs remarked that the little blue speedwell was the prettiest of all the humble roadside flowers. This may surprise many of us who have not looked closely at this low, creeping "gipsy-weed," as it is sometimes called, noting the beauty of its pale blue or lavender flowers. These appear on little spikelike clusters from May to August. This speedwell usually grows in dense mats on dry hillsides, in fields, and in open woods, both at the lower altitudes and up to 5,600 ft.

SH,BR,GS   ⅔ ×   Figwort family

SMOOTH GERARDIA
Gerardia laevigata

In dry woods, especially where oaks predominate, smooth gerardia is a very conspicuous plant from July to September when its bright yellow flowers appear. These are funnel-like or bell-shaped and 1–1½ inches long. The flower buds are round and numerous. The opposite leaves, narrow, sharp-pointed, and variable in outline, are on a smooth green stem 1–3 ft. high. This herb, sometimes called "false yellow foxglove," is known to be partially parasitic on the roots of oaks and other plants. It is fairly common in the southern mountains.

SH,BR,GS   1½ ×   Figwort family

105

Scarlet Painted-Cup
Castilleja coccinea

This handsome species, 10–20 in. high, arises from a basal rosette of hairy leaves. The true flowers are greenish-yellow and practically concealed by vermilion- or scarlet-tinged upper leaves. The latter appear as though the plant had been pulled up and dipped into red paint. Scarlet painted-cup blooms from May to July in wet meadows and moist sandy soils at elevations up to 5,000 ft. It is reputed to be a partial parasite upon the roots of other plants. There are many species of *Castilleja* in the western United States, where they often go by the descriptive name "paint-brush."

BR,GS   1½ ×   Figwort family

Common Lousewort
Pedicularis canadensis

The rather repulsive name of this plant is based on an ancient European fallacy that livestock, after feeding upon a related species *(P. palustris),* became infested with lice. It is also called "wood-betony." Ordinarily common lousewort grows in clusters, with stout hairy stems 8–12 in. tall. The leaves, 3–5 in. long, closely resemble fern leaves and are sometimes mistaken for ferns. Two-lipped, bi-colored flowers are arranged in dense terminal clusters from April to early June. These are usually yellow and reddish-brown or yellow and purplish-brown, and the upper lip is markedly hooded. This common plant grows at elevations up to 3,500 ft. in rather dry woods.

SH,BR,GS   1×   Figwort family

CROSS-VINE   *Bignonia capreolata*

Along the lower streamcourses and in rich moist woods this woody vine is fairly common in the southern mountains where its dark green leaves persist throughout the winter. By means of branched tendrils it may climb into trees to a height of over 50 ft. From April to June cross-vine displays a generous number of very attractive orange and bright yellow bell-shaped flowers—one of our most handsome native plants. Later in the year the long, flat, narrow seed pods are formed, containing numerous winged seeds. A cross-section of the stem reveals a cross-shaped pith, giving rise to its common name.

BR,GS   2½ ×   Bignonia family

BEECH-DROPS   *Epifagus virginiana*

This smooth, slender, naked-appearing plant is parasitic on the roots of beech trees and therefore may be found only where those trees grow. The stems, 6–20 in. high, are stiff branching, and pale yellowish-brown or purplish. A few small, scattered scales take the place of leaves. Flowers are displayed from August to October. These are of two kinds: The mostly sterile upper ones are approximately ⅜ in. long, and the fertile lower ones, about ⅛ in. long. Beech-drops are inconspicuous but fairly common plants whose range extends to 6,000 ft. elevation, the upper limit of beech.

SH,BR,GS   1×   Broom-rape family

107

SQUAWROOT   *Conopholis americana*

The resemblance of this plant to a pine cone is indicated by its generic name, from the Greek *conos,* "cone," and *pholis,* "scale." Ordinarily it grows in clusters, is light brown or tan, and 3–10 in. tall. The stout stalks are covered by stiff overlapping scales instead of leaves. Numerous yellowish flowers, about ½ in. long, are displayed from May to August. These are tubular, two-lipped blossoms from which the stamens protrude very prominently. Squawroot is also called "bear-corn" and "cancer-root." It is a fairly common parasite on the roots of oaks and other trees.

SH,BR,GS   2×   Broom-rape family

ONE-FLOWERED CANCER-ROOT
Orobanche uniflora

Like beech-drops *(Epifagus virginiana)* and squawroot *(Conopholis americana),* one-flowered cancer-root is a member of the Broom-rape family–herbs that lack green foliage, bear scales in place of leaves, and are parasitic on other plants. From a very short stem one-flowered cancer-root sends up 1–4 slender, naked flower stalks 3–8 in. high, each of which bears a single 5-lobed tubular flower. This blossom, ¾–1 in. long, is creamy-white or pale purple, with a coating of very short hairs on the outside. They are delicately fragrant, and bloom from April to June in rich damp woods.

SH,BR,GS   1⅓ ×

Broom-rape family

108

RUELLIA   *Ruellia humilis*

   This is an uncommon to rare wildflower in the Great Smoky Mountains where it grows in dry soils at the lower altitudes. There are no existing records of it along the Blue Ridge Parkway or in Shenandoah National Park. Several pairs of leathery oblong leaves covered with soft white hairs are arranged in opposite fashion along a hairy stem 1–2 ft. high. The showy, funnel-like, blue or lavender flower has 5 nearly equal lobes. These flowers, solitary or in 2's or 3's, appear during the summer. Several forms of this species have been described by botanists.

GS   1½ ×   Acanthus family

PARTRIDGE-BERRY   *Mitchella repens*

   In the dense shade of hemlock forests this low evergreen appears to grow best. There its small, dark green, shining leaves form dense carpets. The opposite leaves are rounded. Paired flowers, united at the base, appear from May to early summer. These are white, waxy, fragrant, 4-lobed, and densely bearded within. Its edible double red fruits persist throughout the winter and were used by Indians as a tonic. This slender-stemmed creeping plant is solely a forest dweller, where it grows from the lower altitudes to 5,200 ft.

SH,BR,GS   1½ ×   Madder family

109

BLUETS   *Houstonia* spp.

Bluets are small spring-blooming wildflowers with opposite smooth-edged leaves and 4-lobed bluish or purplish flowers. What some of the various species lack in size they make up for by their profusion. This is the case with the little thyme-leaved bluet *(H. serpyllifolia)* of the Blue Ridge Parkway and Great Smoky Mountains, which carpets the high-altitude road banks in late spring with extensive mats of lovely blue. At lower elevations, in open grassy habitats, the similar "Quaker-ladies" *(H. caerulea* shown top) is fairly common. The other species of bluets have clustered, instead of single, flowers, and their 4-lobed blossoms have a less pronounced flare. These include the purple *(H. purpurea* shown below), slender- leaved *(H. tenuifolia),* and long-leaved bluets *(H. longifolia).*

SH,BR,GS   top 1⅓ ×; bottom 2×   Madder family

110

BUSH-HONEYSUCKLE   *Diervilla sessilifolia*

In the Canadian Zone forests of the southern mountains this common shrub grows in openings at elevations from 4,000 to 6,500 ft. It was discovered there by Samuel B. Buckley more than a century ago, one of 24 new species of plants found by this companion of Arnold Guyot; both Buckley and Guyot are honored in the names of two high mountains in the Great Smokies. Bush-honeysuckle is usually 2–6 ft. high with a branching reddish stem. The leaves are opposite, stemless, toothed along the margins, and measure 2–5 in. long. Yellowish-green flowers are displayed from June to August.

BR,GS   1⅓ ×   Honeysuckle family

JAPANESE HONEYSUCKLE   *Lonicera japonica*

While the delightful odor given off by the flowers of this Asiatic vine makes it a great favorite in some places, the engulfing of young forests by this fast-growing evergreen climber places it in the category of a noxious weed. Japanese honeysuckle has been known to grow as much as 30 ft. in a year. The glossy, evergreen, opposite leaves are readily eaten by cattle and deer. The white or pinkish flowers appear from May to early summer but soon fade. Scattered blossoms appear throughout the season.

SH,BR,GS   4×   Honeysuckle family

111

TRUMPET HONEYSUCKLE
Lonicera sempervirens

This handsome woody vine is common in Shenandoah National Park but scarce in the mountains to the south. In the Great Smokies it is believed to be an escape from cultivation. The opposite oval leaves are dark green above and pale beneath; the upper 1 or 2 pairs are united and appear to be pierced by the stem. Slender, trumpet-shaped flowers appear in late April or May, arranged in 2 or 3 whorls. The little trumpets, 1–1½ in. long, are a bright scarlet on the outside and yellow within. The fruit is a small red berry. This slender twining vine, also called "coral honeysuckle," grows in woods and along fence rows at the lower altitudes.

SH,BR,GS   1⅓ ×
Honeysuckle family

CORALBERRY
Symphoricarpos orbiculatus

The dense clusters of small, round, coral-pink berries on this shrub persist long after the leaves fall, and therefore it is popular in cultivation in some areas. As it often escapes from places where it was planted, it may be difficult to determine whether it is or is not native. It forms dense thickets, and it has been used effectively in sterile soils as a means of erosion control. The opposite, oval-shaped leaves have minute hairs on the underside. Small bell-shaped flowers are produced mostly in July and August. It grows 2–6 ft. high along roadsides, in disturbed areas, and at the edges of woodlands.

SH,BR,GS   1½ ×
Honeysuckle family

HOBBLEBUSH   *Viburnum alnifolium*

In moist shaded ravines this irregularly branching shrub may occur at elevations as low as 3,000 ft., but ordinarily it grows well above that altitude in cool moist forests. The large, round, opposite leaves have prominent veins and saw-toothed margins. These begin to turn color in mid-summer and display variegated hues until the autumn frosts. Showy blossoms occur from April to June, arranged in flat-topped terminal clusters with large, chalky-white, 5-rayed, neutral flowers (lacking stamens and pistils) along the margins. The oval-shaped fruits become red and finally dark purple or almost black. Hobblebush is also called "witch-hobble."

BR,GS   top 2×; bottom 3×   Honeysuckle family

MAPLE-LEAVED VIBURNUM
Viburnum acerifolium

The leaves of this fairly common shrub resemble those of red maple (*Acer rubrum*) in shape, size, and in their opposite placement on the branches. On occasion one must examine the plant closely in order to be sure of a correct identification. In late summer and autumn, however, the flat-topped clusters of fleshy purplish-black fruits make recognition relatively easy. Also at that time of year the leaf colors—lilac, violet, magenta, or pale rose—make this shrub one of the loveliest of all our woody plants. Cream-colored clusters of flowers, 1–3 in. across, are borne from May to early July.

SH,BR,GS   2×   Honeysuckle family

RED-BERRIED ELDER
Sambucus pubens

Flowers of the red-berried elder are pyramidal (as in the lilac) and the ripe fruits are bright red. In the American elder (*S. canadensis*) the flowers are arranged in larger, flat-topped clusters, and the ripe fruits are purplish-black. The fruits of the former shrub are inedible while those of the latter are agreeable to the taste. Stems of red-berried elder have a brown pith, while those of American elder have a white pith. Red-berried elder is most common at high altitudes where it flowers in May and June; and in July its bright red fruit clusters are very showy.

SH,BR,GS   2×   Honeysuckle family

VENUS'S LOOKING-GLASS
Specularia perfoliata

The small, rounded, clasping leaves of this plant look like so many green shells cupped around the stem. The rather weak, slender stem, 6–24 in. tall, is angled and quite hairy. Stemless violet-blue flowers appear at the base of some of the upper leaves from May to August, and are usually solitary, although 2 or 3 may be together. The deeply incised 5-lobed flower is ½–¾ in. across. Venus's looking-glass ordinarily grows in waste places where the soil is dry and relatively sterile.

SH,BR,GS   1×   Bluebell family

TALL BELLFLOWER
Campanula americana

Unlike the other native bluebells, or bellflowers, this species has a flat, star-shaped flower. These blue flowers, approximately 1 in. across, are arranged along a terminal leafy spike from June to August. From the center of the deeply 5-cleft flower there projects a very prominent style which droops and then turns upward, extending well out from the mouth of the flower. The thin, long-pointed, willowlike leaves are 3–6 in. long with toothed margins. The tall bellflower grows in moist woods at the lowest altitudes to about 3,000 ft.

SH,BR,GS   1×   Bluebell family

115

SOUTHERN HAREBELL
Campanula divaricata

During the summer the numerous, small, light blue bells of this common wildflower nod from slender loosely branched stems. Within the 5-lobed flower are 5 stamens and a single long-protruding style which resembles an exceptionally long clapper in a miniature (¼–⅓ in. long) bell. The leaves are alternate, pointed at both ends, and 2–3 in. long. This "panicled bellflower," as it is sometimes called, is a common plant along trails and roadsides and in fairly dry places where it grows at the low to middle altitudes.

SH,BR,GS   1⅓ ×   Bluebell family

CARDINAL-FLOWER
Lobelia cardinalis

During the latter half of the summer the tall, erect stems of cardinal-flower display their brilliant red or vermilion flowers and become hosts to the hummingbirds. The lower lip of the blossom has 3 very prominent lobes; the upper lip, 2 smaller ones. Beneath the flower spike are numerous dark green leaves pointed at both ends. This is the only red-flowered species of *Lobelia* in the Southern Appalachians; the others are bluish or purplish. It grows along streamsides, in roadside ditches, in marshes and wet meadows at the lowest altitudes to over 3,500 ft.

SH,BR,GS   6×   Bluebell family

GREAT LOBELIA   *Lobelia siphilitica*

Like its more brilliantly colored relative, cardinal-flower *(L. cardinalis)*, this lobelia displays its blossoms in the summer and grows along streamsides and in wet places. The 2-lipped flowers, which may be dark blue, light blue, violet, and occasionally pinkish or white, are borne on a leafy spike. This common stout-stemmed plant may be 1–3 ft. tall. The leaves are alternate, pointed at both ends, and 2–6 in. long. In times past this lobelia was reputed to be effective in the treatment of syphilis, thus accounting for its specific name. A smaller cousin, "Indian-tobacco" *(L. inflata)*, is being used in preparations aimed at arresting the use of tobacco.

SH,BR,GS   3×   Bluebell family

NEW YORK IRONWEED
Vernonia noveboracensis

In late July or early August New York ironweed blooms, a reminder that summer is at the halfway mark and that the pageantry of goldenrods, asters, and coloring leaves is soon to begin. This erect leafy-stemmed plant grows 3–9 ft. tall in low wet meadows, along streamsides, and in moist soil at the lower altitudes. Its numerous willowlike leaves have toothed margins and are 3–10 in. long. Each plant consists of many heads of purple or rose-purple flowers, there being 20 or more small, tubular blossoms in each cluster. The aggregate of flower heads tends to appear flat-topped.

SH,BR,GS   3×   Composite family

117

PURPLE JOE-PYE-WEED
Eupatorium purpureum

Joe Pye is said to have been an herb doctor who lived in New England in colonial times, when the colonists made a tonic of these roots to treat diarrhea. The plant named for him is hardly, a "weed" in the ordinary sense as it is one of our most stately and handsome herbs. A more fitting name, "queen-of-the-meadow," is applied to it in the southern mountains. Some of these plants reach a height of 12 ft. or more in low moist ground. The large, coarsely toothed leaves are arranged in whorls along the stem, with 3 to 6 leaves per whorl. The numerous flower clusters (July–September) are grouped into a huge, frosty-pink, rounded or pyramidal head.

SH,BR,GS   20×   Composite family

BONESET   *Eupatorium perfoliatum*

Like its relative Joe-Pye-weed *(E. purpureum),* this herb grows in wet meadows and marshlands, where it blossoms in late summer. It is comparatively drab-looking with numerous dull-white flower heads arranged in a dense and somewhat flattened terminal cluster. The opposite, tough, long-pointed leaves have saw-toothed margins and a wrinkled appearance. Except for a few of the upper pairs, these leaves are united and encircle the 2–4-ft. main stem. "Boneset tea," made from the dried leaves of this plant, was a well-known tonic of past generations.

SH,BR,GS   2×   Composite family

118

WHITE SNAKEROOT
Eupatorium rugosum

While the flower head of this plant resembles a white ageratum, its somewhat heart-shaped or triangular leaves are so similar to those of the nettle *(Urtica)* that it was formerly known as "nettle-leaved thoroughwort" *(E. urticaefolium)*. It is a very common plant in rich woodlands at high altitudes where it displays its snow-white flower clusters in August and September. Opposite, coarsely toothed leaves are arranged along a slender stem 1–4 ft. tall. Fatal cases of "milk-sickness" in man have been traced to the use of milk from cows that had eaten white snakeroot. It is sometimes poisonous to cattle.

SH,BR,GS   2× Composite family

BLAZING-STAR   *Liatris spicata*

In some localities this very attractive plant is fairly common, but for the most part it is rather scarce in these areas. The stem, 2–5 ft. tall, bears numerous long, narrow leaves, the lower ones up to 12 in. or more in length. In August and September the rose-purple flowers appear in densely compacted spikes 5–15 in. long. Another name for this handsome plant is "button-snakeroot," from its globular roots. Other names include "gayfeather," "devil's-bit," and "rattlesnake-master." It grows on wet slopes and in marshes and other moist places.

SH,BR,GS   20×   Composite family

MARYLAND GOLDEN-ASTER
Chrysopsis mariana

Many a dry, exposed hillside is enlivened in August and September by the bright, golden flower heads of this plant. The stem, 1–2 ft. high, is covered with silky hairs which usually disappear in the mature specimen. The alternate, oblong leaves are neither toothed nor lobed. The smaller upper ones are stemless, while the larger lower leaves possess leaf stems. The Composite family, to which this golden-aster belongs, is characterized by its numerous small flowers crowded together into one or more heads, in contrast to such familiar single flowers as the violet or buttercup.

BR.GS   2×   Composite family

GOLDENROD   *Solidago* spp.

Of the more than 100 species of goldenrods growing in North America, over 24 may be found in these eastern mountains (20 in the Great Smokies alone). As a plant genus, goldenrods are difficult to identify because they tend to hybridize. All except a single white-flowered species *(S. bicolor)* have yellow flowers. Some may be regarded as "weeds." Goldenrods have alternate leaves, starting with a large basal rosette. Some species begin to flower in early summer, and a number continue to bloom until frost. They grow in a wide variety of habitats.

SH,BR,GS   10×   Composite family

WHITE GOLDENROD   *Solidago bicolor*

Except for this white-flowered species, goldenrods of the eastern mountains are yellow or gold. "Silver-rod," as the species is sometimes called, is a stiff-stemmed plant 1–4 ft. tall. White goldenrod grows in dry soils from the lowest altitudes to 6,300 ft. There are more than 10,000 species of plants in the Composite family to which the goldenrods belong, including asters, sunflowers, thistles, dandelions, hawkweeds, and others.

SH,BR,GS   2×   Composite family

WHITE WOOD ASTER   *Aster divaricatus*

Since they are inclined to hybridize rather freely, asters, like goldenrods, may present identification problems. Beginners, especially, encounter difficulties with the numerous, slightly-differing races, some of which are often described as distinct species. In each of the three areas covered by this book there are at least 20 kinds of asters. The highly variable white wood aster has a somewhat zigzag stem 1–3 ft. tall and thin, saw-toothed leaves. The flower heads, ¾–1 in. across, consist of 6–9 white, petal-like rays arranged around a brown central disk. It grows in fairly dry woods where the blossoms appear in September and October.

SH,BR,GS   1½ ×   Composite family

121

LARGE-LEAVED ASTER
Aster macrophyllus

The Greek word for "star," *aster,* is both a scientific and a common name. Asters are cosmopolitan in their distribution, growing in a variety of habitats from near sea level to the summits of the highest eastern mountains. Large-leaved aster, usually 2–3 ft. high, has rather thick, saw-toothed leaves, the lower ones being large and heart-shaped. The yellow-centered flower heads, ½– 1½ in. across, have approximately 16 petal-like rays which may be lavender, pale purple, or violet. It grows in dry, shaded places where it blooms in the late summer and early autumn.

SH,BR,GS　　2×　　Composite family

HEART-LEAVED ASTER
Aster cordifolius

"Frostflowers," as asters are sometimes called, have alternate leaves and flower heads with petal-like rays which may be white, pink, purple, blue, or violet. Ordinarily the central disk is yellow, later turning red, brown, or purple. Heart-leaved or "common blue" aster has a much-branched, bushy appearance, the main stem reaching 5 ft. or more in height on occasion. It is a handsome plant with numerous small flowers ½–¾ in. across. These have 10–20 petal-like, pale blue or violet rays. It blossoms in woods and along shaded roadsides throughout the autumn.

SH,BR,GS　　　　　　　1×　　　　　　Composite family

ROBIN'S-PLANTAIN   *Erigeron pulchellus*

This common asterlike plant is one of the earliest members of the Composite family to come into bloom, its first flowers appearing in late March at lower altitudes in the southern mountains. The stem of this plant, 8–20 in. tall, is soft, hollow, and, like the leaves, is covered with long thin hairs. The basal leaves, 1–3 in. long, are oval or widened at one end. The stem leaves are alternate and partly clasping. Numerous (about 50) 1–1½ in. petal-like rays, bluish-purple or violet, encircle the yellow central disk. Robin's-plantain grows at elevations up to 5,500 ft.

SH,BR,GS   3×   Composite family

PLANTAIN-LEAVED PUSSY'S-TOES
Antennaria plantaginifolia

It is not unusual to find the early flowers on this common plant before the last snowfall has melted. Staminate (male) and pistillate (female) plants grow separately; the former are smaller, with more highly colored flowers. The latter flowers resemble white conical tassels of silk. The basal leaves, 1½–3 in. long, are dull dark green above and silvery beneath. Plantain-leaved pussy's-toes, also called "everlasting," "mouse-ear," and "ladies'-tobacco," is covered with a soft down and grows in extensive colonies, spreading by means of runners. It grows 3–18 in. tall on dry open slopes and in rocky meadows.

SH,BR,GS   3×   Composite family

Catfoot *Gnaphalium obtusifolium*

The stem, undersurface of the leaves, and base of the bracts enclosing the flower clusters are covered with wool-like hairs. The blossoms, displayed from August to October, are white or cream-colored and arranged in many-flowered heads. Narrow, stemless leaves are usually dark green above. It is sometimes called "poverty-weed" and "old-field balsam," because it thrives in dry areas and waste places. Names such as "sweet balsam" and "sweet life-everlasting" refer to its fragrance. Other names are "rabbit-tobacco" and "cudweed."

SH,BR,GS   4×   Composite family

Common ragweed
Ambrosia artemisiifolia

Probably none of our native plants is more despised than this common pernicious weed, the chief cause of hay fever in late summer. Many regard this plant as the outstanding example of a so-called weed growing in cultivated ground to the detriment of crops, an economically valueless and unsightly plant. Common ragweed, also called "Roman wormwood," "hog-weed," and "bitter-weed," has deeply divided fernlike leaves and inconspicuous heads of greenish flowers. A coarse plant 1–3 ft. tall, it grows abundantly along roadsides, in cultivated fields, in gardens, and elsewhere.

SH,BR,GS   3×   Composite family

OX-EYE   *Heliopsis helianthoides*

Sometimes known as the "false sunflower," oxe-eye resembles sunflowers quite closely. A smooth stem 3–5 ft. high supports showy heads of rayed flowers (July–September) about 2 in. across, each with 10 or more bright-yellow rays. The thin leaves are usually paired and opposite, with occasionally 3 in a whorl. These are 3–6 in. long and 1–2 in. wide, with toothed margins. Ox-eye is often found along streams and in moist soils. The more common black-eyed susan *(Rudbeckia hirta)* which ox-eye also closely resembles is a shorter plant with a hairy stem, narrower leaves, and a darker-colored central disk.

SH,BR,GS   2×   Composite family

CUTLEAF CONEFLOWER   *Rudbeckia laciniata*

This relative of the more familiar black-eyed susan *(R. hirta)* is a smoother, taller-growing, much-branched plant with leaves that are prominently divided and lobed, and with a much taller flower disk. Cutleaf coneflower, also called "tall" or "green-headed coneflower," is a very common herb along streams and in the moist, rich forests at high altitudes (to 6,500 ft.) in the Southern Appalachian Mountains. Here its showy golden-yellow flowers are displayed from July to September. On occasions it grows to a height of 10 ft. or over.

SH,BR,GS   15×   Composite family

125

BLACK-EYED SUSAN *Rudbeckia hirta*

This very common to abundant plant is a popular wildflower but can also be an obnoxious weed. It is said to come from the plains and prairies of the western states where it is native. Along roadsides, in open fields, and elsewhere it grows from the lowest altitudes to 5,000 ft. Usually 1–2 ft. high, black-eyed susan has stems and leaves that are rough and hairy. Showy flower heads with orange-yellow petal-like rays and purplish-brown disks in the center are displayed from June to August. It is also called "yellow daisy."

SH,BR,GS   5×   Composite family

SUNFLOWER *Helianthus* spp.

Sunflowers are coarse annuals or perennials whose yellow-rayed flowers are conspicuously displayed in summer or early autumn. In addition to approximately 100 species in the genus *Helianthus* (true sunflowers) there are a number of related genera with many kinds of sunflowerlike flowers. About 6 species of true sunflowers grow in each of the 3 mountain parks described in this book. Narrow-leaved sunflower (*H. angustifolius*) is readily identified by its extremely narrow, stemless leaves that are alternately arranged along the upper part of the slender stem but in opposite manner along the lower part. Its showy yellow flowers often grow in large masses in moist ground.

SH,BR,GS   4×   Composite family

CROWN-BEARD
Verbesina occidentalis

Even when at its peak of flowering this tall-growing herb (3–7 ft. high) has a very disheveled appearance, its 2–5 yellow rays set in a decidedly irregular manner about the flower head. This character, along with its prominently 4-winged stem, identifies it. The thin opposite leaves, 4–8 in. long, are sharp-pointed, with saw-toothed margins. Ordinarily it is a much-branched plant that grows in open woods and on dry hillsides, where it flowers in August and September. There are no records of its occurrence in Shenandoah National Park, but it is locally abundant along the Blue Ridge Parkway and in the Great Smoky Mountains.

BR,GS   4×   Composite family

TALL COREOPSIS   *Coreopsis major*

Tall coreopsis, also called "tickseed," is a slender-stemmed plant whose blossoms resemble those of a small sunflower and the closely related "beggar-tricks" *(Bidens)*. This coreopsis has a stem 2–3 ft. tall topped (June–August) by several to many flower heads. These are 1–2 in. across, with 6–10 (mostly 8) yellow rays. The opposite leaves are divided at the base into 3 willowlike leaflets which have the appearance of a whorl of 6 leaves. Tall coreopsis grows at elevations up to 5,000 ft. in dry, open woods and along trails and roadsides.

SH,BR,GS   3×   Composite family

127

AUTUMN SNEEZEWEED   *Helenium autumnale*

Swamps and low, wet meadows are the usual habitat of the autumn sneezeweed, which is also called "swamp sunflower." In such places it has been considered an obnoxious weed, but in the highlands it is ordinarily uncommon. The stout, branching stems, 2–6 ft. tall, are aromatic and resinous. They look winged because the bases of the bright green leaves run along the stem. Numerous flower heads are displayed from August to October. These somewhat resemble coneflowers *(Rudbeckia)*. Sneezing may be induced by the pollen or by smelling the dry pulverized leaves.

BR,GS   2×   Composite family

COMMON YARROW
Achillea millefolium

Although common yarrow and wild carrot *(Daucus carota)* are not related, these plants are often mistaken for each other. Both are about the same size, bloom at the same time, have flat-topped heads of white flowers, and have finely-divided leaves. Both are of European origin and, on occasions, become obnoxious weeds. Yarrow flowers are a dull white and not lacelike as in the wild carrot, and the rootstock is horizontal and not turniplike. Yarrow or "milfoil," was formerly used as a tonic and in the cure of various ailments. It grows along roadsides and in fields and waste places, where it flowers during the summer.

SH,BR,GS   1×   Composite family

128

OX-EYE-DAISY   *Chrysanthemum leucanthemum*

It may surprise some of us to learn that the familiar and abundant ox-eye-daisy is indeed a *Chrysanthemum,* related to the big, spectacular round-headed "mums" grown by florists. *Chrysanthemum* is a Greek name meaning "golden flower" whereas the species name *leucanthemum* means "white flower," both colors being attractively combined in this handsome emigrant from the Old World. While the farmer may look upon this "white-weed" as a pest, others regard this common plant as being one of our loveliest flowers. Ox-eye daisy blooms from May until the autumn frosts.

SH,BR,GS   5×   Composite family

PALE INDIAN-PLANTAIN
Cacalia atriplicifolia

From middle July until September, when pale Indian-plantain is in bloom, this plant displays its flat-topped terminal clusters of white or yellowish-green flowers on stems that are often 5 to 7 ft. high. It is then a conspicuous roadside herb, especially along the Skyline Drive and in some localities along the Blue Ridge Parkway. The leaves of "wild caraway," as it is sometimes called, are green above and whitish beneath. Along the lower portion of the tall stem the leaves are quite large. With their irregular lobes and teeth they look like sycamore *(Platanus)* leaves.

SH,BR,GS   3×   Composite family

SMALL'S RAGWORT   *Senecio smallii*

Ragworts are also called "groundsel" and "squaw-weed." The more generally distributed species grow 12–24 in. tall and resemble small yellow-rayed daisies with 8–12 petal-like rays. In the eastern mountains 3 species are quite common: golden ragwort *(S. aureus),* with heart-shaped basal leaves; round-leaved squaw-weed *(S. obovatus),* with rounded or broadened basal leaves; and Small's ragwort *(S. smallii),* with linear-oblong basal leaves. The first two species flower early in the spring. The third, which is the most common, colors extensive meadows with gold in May and June.

BR,GS   3×   Composite family

BULL THISTLE   *Cirsium vulgare*

Of the 5 thistles *(Cirsium* spp.) in the southern mountains this species and Canada thistle *(C. arvense)* are natives of Europe. The bull thistle grows 3–5 ft. tall; the stem is thick, rough, and leafy. The dark green, deeply lobed leaves are wooly-gray beneath, tipped with sharp prickles. Handsome heads of purple or pink flowers, 2–3 in. across, are borne from July until frost. In the southern parts of the eastern mountains thistles are rather uncommon, but to the north these colorful spiny plants may become aggressive weeds. They grow along roadsides and in pastures and waste places.

SH,BR,GS   2×   Composite family

SPOTTED STAR-THISTLE   *Centaurea maculosa*

This European immigrant grows in extensive patches along roadsides in Shenandoah National Park, but there is no record of its occurrence in the Great Smokies. From late June until early autumn this close relative of "blue cornflower" or "bachelor's-button" *(C. cyanus)* displays purplish-pink flower heads approximately 1 in. across. The much-branched stem, 1–4 ft. tall, is slender and wiry, and the narrowly divided leaves are covered with small white hairs. Spotted star-thistle is also known as "spotted knapweed." It grows in fields and waste places.

SH,BR   1×   Composite family

COMMON CHICORY
Cichorium intybus

Like the ox-eye-daisy *(Chrysanthemum leucanthemum)* this European immigrant is both a handsome plant and a noxious weed. Few, if any, wildflowers have blossoms of such superb shade of blue. These may appear in June, with some still to be found in October. The flower heads unfold their 12–20 square tipped petal-like rays at sunrise and close them about noon. On cloudy or rainy days the flowers usually remain closed. The long taproot is dried, ground, and added to coffee to improve its flavor. While the stem leaves are quite small and clasping, the rosette of basal leaves somewhat resembles that of the dandelion. Common chicory grows along roadsides, in old fields, and waste places.

SH,BR,GS   1×   Composite family

131

DWARF DANDELION   *Krigia biflora*

The smooth stem of this little herb, 8–24 in. tall, bears 1–6 orange or orange-red flower heads and resembles the related hawkweeds *(Hieracium)*. One to 3 oblong or oval leaves clasp the stem. The basal leaves, 2–7 in. long, have winged stems. Dwarf dandelion grows in moist woods and meadows where it flowers from May to August. The generic name of this plant honors David Krieg, a German physician and botanist who was one of the first plant collectors in Maryland. Shenandoah National Park reports an annual species, *K. virginica.*

BR,GS   ⅔ ×

Composite family

RATTLESNAKE-ROOT
Prenanthes altissima

Rattlesnake-root is said to have been used in treating snake bites, the leaves were steeped in water and applied as a poultice. "Gall-of-the-earth," another name for this plant, refers to its intensely bitter roots. This tall (3–7 ft.) herb is characterized by the extreme variation in its leaves (lobed and divided, oval, triangular, heart-shaped, etc.) and by the wandlike clusters of nodding, somewhat bell-shaped flowers which are yellowish or greenish-white. Flowering occurs July–October. It is a common plant in moist woods.

SH,BR,GS   2×   Composite family

MOUSE-EAR *Hieracium pilosella*

This is another of the several hawkweeds that have come to us from Europe, where overly zealous botanists have described hundreds of "subspecies" of this variable plant. It is a dwarf herb, its stem rarely over 10 in. tall. The practically leafless stem usually bears a solitary yellow flower approximately 1 in. across, but on rare occasions 2 or 3 flowers may be displayed. Blossoms are found from May to September. The name "mouse-ear" comes from the small earlike clump of hairy basal leaves. It spreads rapidly by means of strawberrylike runners as well as by seeds. A silken appendage attached to the seeds enables them to be borne by the wind for considerable distances.

SH,BR,GS   2×   Composite family

FIELD HAWKWEED *Hieracium pratense*

Ten of the 19 species of hawkweeds included in *Gray's Manual of Botany* (1950) for the northeastern quarter of the United States are of European origin. Among these immigrants, most of which are obnoxious weeds, is field hawkweed, or "king-devil." It is plentiful in Shenandoah National Park and the northern Blue Ridge Parkway, where its yellow flowers account for golden masses of roadside color in June, but it is not among the 6 species of hawkweeds known to grow in the Great Smokies. It flowers from May to September. These flowers close at night.

SH,BR   4×   Composite family

133

SUGGESTED READINGS

Information on specific areas, more complete information on the flowers listed, or more complete coverage of the areas included in this book may be found among the following selected references.

CAMPBELL, C. C. *et al. Great Smoky Mountains Wildflowers.* Knoxville, Tenn.: University of Tennessee Press, 1964.

FERNALD, MERRITT L. *Gray's Manual of Botany.* 8th ed. New York: American Book Co., 1950.

GLEASON, HENRY A. *Illustrated Flora of the Northeastern United States and Canada. (The New Britton and Brown.)* 3 vols. New York Botanical Gardens, 1952.

GRIMM, WILLIAM C. *The Book of Shrubs.* Harrisburg, Penn.: Stackpole Co., 1957.

LEMMON, ROBERT S. and JOHNSON, CHARLES C. *Wildflowers of North America.* Garden City, N.Y.: Hanover House, 1961.

LORD, WILLIAM G. *The Blue Ridge Parkway Guide.* 4 vols. Asheville, N.C.: Stephens Press, 1939 to 1963.

MASSEY, A. B. *Virginia Flora.* (An annotated plant catalog. Technical Bulletin 155.) Blacksburg, Va.: Virginia Agricultural Experiment Station, 1961.

RICKETT, H. W. *Wild Flowers of America.* New York: Crown Publishers, Inc., 1953.

SHARPE, GRANT and WENONAH. *101 Wildflowers of Shenandoah National Park*. Seattle, Wash.: University of Washington Press, 1958.

STRAUSBAUGH, P. D., and CORE, EARL L. *Flora of West Virginia*. 4 vols. (West Virginia University Bulletin, Series 52.) Morgantown, W. Va.: West Virginia University, 1952 to 1964.

STUPKA, ARTHUR. *Trees, Shrubs, and Woody Vines of Great Smoky Mountains National Park*. Knoxville, Tenn.: University of Tennessee Press, 1964.

WHERRY, EDGAR T. *Wild Flower Guide, Eastern and Midland United States*. New York: Doubleday & Co., Inc., 1954.

ZIM, HERBERT, and MARTIN, ALEXANDER C. *Flowers*. (A Golden Nature Guide.) New York: Golden Press, 1950.

INDEX

COLOR INDEX

Flowers illustrated in this book are listed here by color, simple common name, and page. Where a flower may occur in two or more colors, or where there may be divergence of opinion as to the color, it will be listed under each color possibility. Bicolor flowers are listed under the bicolor heading, but also under each of the colors represented if there is no one predominate color.